SPECIAL-DAY CALENDAR CARDS

Grandma Moses' Birthday

Citizenship Day

Ice-Cream Cone Day

Grandparents' Day

Tomie De Paola's Birthday

Fabulous Fall Day

Labor Day

Nature Day

Football Day

SPECIAL-DAY CALENDAR CARDS

Native American Day

Harvest Moon Day

Johnny Appleseed Day

Good-Neighbor Day

Muppet Day

National Fishing Day

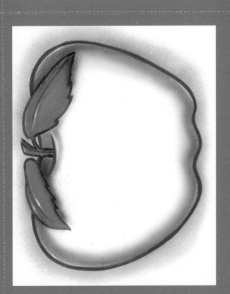

Celebrate the Months
SEPTEMBER

EDITOR:

Joellyn Thrall Cicciarelli

ILLUSTRATORS:

David Christensen

Darcy Tom

Jane Yamada

PROJECT DIRECTOR:

Carolea Williams

CONTRIBUTING WRITERS:

Trisha Callella	Kim Jordano
Rosa Drew	Mary Kurth
Marguerite Duke	Melissa Mangan
Ronda Howley	Jody Vogel

TABLE OF CONTENTS

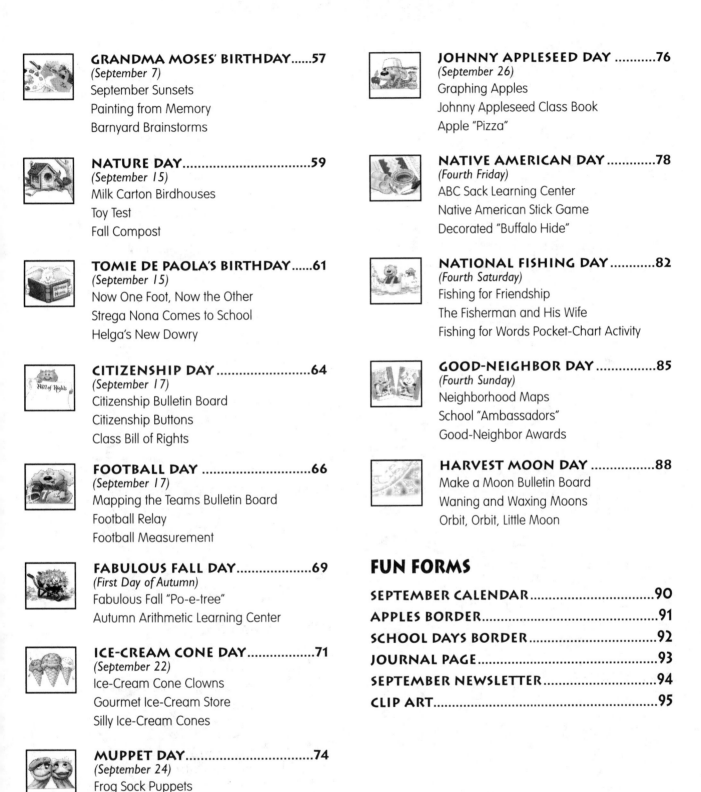

FUN FORMS

INTRODUCTION

Seasons, holidays, annual events, and just-for-fun monthly themes provide fitting frameworks for learning! Celebrate September and its special days with these exciting and unique activities. This activity book of integrated curriculum ideas includes the following:

MONTHLY CELEBRATION THEMES

▲ **monthly celebration activities** that relate to monthlong and weeklong events or themes, such as Back to School, Apples, and National Literacy Month.

▲ **literature lists** of fiction and nonfiction books for each monthly celebration.

▲ **bulletin-board displays** that can be used for seasonal decoration and interactive learning-center fun.

▲ **take-home activities** to reinforce what is being taught in school, encourage home–school communication, and help children connect home and school learning.

SPECIAL-DAY THEMES

▲ **special-day activities** that relate to 15 special September days, including Labor Day, Football Day, and Johnny Appleseed Day. Activities integrate art, songs and chants, language arts, math, science, and social studies.

▲ **calendar cards** that complement each of the 15 special days and add some extra seasonal fun to your daily calendar time.

▲ **literature lists** of fiction and nonfiction books for each special day.

FUN FORMS

▲ a **blank monthly calendar** for writing lesson plans, dates to remember, special events, book titles, new words and incentives, or for math and calendar activities.

▲ **seasonal border pages** that add eye-catching appeal to parent notes, homework assignments, letters, certificates, announcements, and bulletins.

▲ **seasonal journal pages** for students to share thoughts, feelings, stories, or experiences. Reproduce and bind several pages for individual journals or combine single, completed journal pages to make a class book.

▲ a **classroom newsletter** for students to report current classroom events and share illustrations, comics, stories, or poems. Reproduce and send completed newsletters home to keep families informed and involved.

▲ **clip art** to add a seasonal flair to bulletin boards, class projects, charts, and parent notes.

SPECIAL-DAY CALENDAR CARD ACTIVITIES

Below are a variety of ways to introduce special-day calendar cards into your curriculum.

PATTERNING

During daily calendar time, use one of these patterning activities to reinforce students' math skills.

▲ Use special-day calendar cards and your own calendar markers to create a pattern for the month, such as regular day, regular day, special day.

▲ Number special-day cards in advance. Use only even- or odd-numbered special days for patterning. (Create your own "special days" with the blank calendar cards.) Use your own calendar markers to create the other half of the pattern.

▲ At the beginning of the month, attach the special-day cards to the calendar. Use your own calendar markers for patterning. When a special day arrives, invite a student to remove the special-day card and replace it with your calendar marker to continue the pattern.

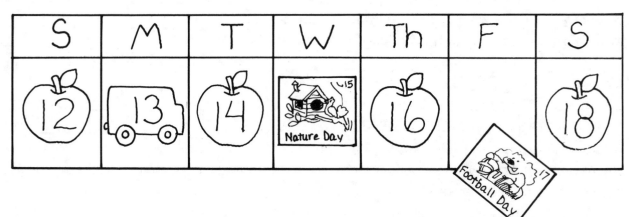

HIDE AND FIND

On the first day of the month, hide numbered special-day cards around the classroom. Invite students to find them and bring them to the calendar area. Have a student volunteer hang each card in the correct calendar space as you explain the card's significance.

A FESTIVE INTRODUCTION

On the first day of the month, display special-day cards in a festive setting, such as a fall leaf display. Invite students, one at a time, to remove a card and attach it to the calendar as you explain its significance.

POCKET-CHART SENTENCE STRIPS

On the first day of the month, have the class dictate a sentence to correspond with each special-day card. For example, on Nature Day you might write *On this special day, we celebrate the protection of the earth and animals.* Put the sentence strips away. When a special day arrives, place the corresponding strip in a pocket chart next to the calendar. Move a fun "pointer" (such as a pencil with a paper earth taped to it) under the words, and have students read the sentence aloud. Add sentences to the pocket chart on each special day.

GUESS WHAT I HAVE

Discuss the special days and give each student a photocopy of one of the special-day cards. (Two or three students may have the same card.) Have students take turns describing their card without revealing the special day. For example, a student may say *This is the day we celebrate all the people who work in this country.* Invite the student who guesses Labor Day to attach the card to the calendar.

TREAT BAGS

Place each special-day card and a small corresponding treat or prize in a resealable plastic bag. For example, place a leaf in a bag for Fabulous Fall Day. On the first day of the month, pin the bags on a bulletin board near the calendar. Remove the special-day cards from the bags and attach them to the calendar as you discuss each day. As a special day arrives, remove and explain the corresponding bag's contents. Choose a student to keep the contents as a special reward.

LITERATURE MATCHUP

Have students sit in two lines facing each other. Provide the members of one group with special-day cards and the members of the other group with books whose subjects match the special-day cards held by the other group. Invite students to match cards and books, come forward in pairs, and introduce the day and book. Display the books near the calendar for students to read.

MINI-BOOKS

Reproduce numbered special-day cards so each student has a set. Have students sequence and staple their cards to make mini-books. Invite students to read the books and take them home to share with family members.

CREATIVE WRITING

Have each student glue a copy of a special-day card to a piece of construction paper. Invite students to illustrate and write about the special day. Have students share their writing. Display the writing near the calendar.

LUNCH SACK GAME

Provide each student with a paper lunch sack, a photocopy of each special-day card, and 15 index cards. Have students decorate the sacks for the month. Invite students to color the special-day cards and write on separate index cards a word or sentence describing each day. Have students place the special-day cards and index cards in the sacks. Ask students to trade sacks, empty the contents, and match index cards to special-day cards.

SPECIAL-DAY BOX

One week before a special day, provide each student with a photocopied special-day card, an empty check box or shoe box, and a four-page square blank book. Ask each student to take the box, book, and card home to prepare a special-day box presentation. Have students write about their special day on the four book pages and place in the box small pictures or artifacts relating to the day. Ask students to decorate the boxes and glue their special-day cards to the top. Have students bring the completed boxes to school on the special day and give their presentations as an introduction to the day.

BACK TO SCHOOL

It's back to school and back to fun with these exciting activities! These fun, educational "glad you're back" activities welcome your students, help you prepare for the year ahead, and get everything off to a great start!

LITERATURE LINKS

Alice Ann Gets Ready for School
by Cynthia Jabar

*The Berenstain Bears
Go to School*
by Stan and Jan Berenstain

*A Hippopotamus Ate the
Teacher*
by Mike Thaler

*John Patrick Morman
McHennessy—The Boy Who
Was Always Late*
by John Burningham

School
by Emily Arnold McCully

School Bus
by Donald Crews

Starting School
by Janet and Allen Ahlberg

This Is the Way We Go to School
by Edith Bayer

"GUESS WHO" BULLETIN BOARD

Have students use crayons or markers, art supplies, and scissors to decorate and cut out a paper doll that represents themselves. Ask each student to turn the paper doll over and write his or her name (upside down) on the doll's back near the feet. Staple the dolls, top halves only, to a bulletin board titled *Guess Who's in Your Class This Year!* During free time, invite students to look at the dolls, guess who they represent, and flip up the legs and read the names on the back to check their guesses.

MATERIALS

▲ Paper Doll reproducible (page 17)
▲ crayons or markers
▲ art supplies (glue, wallpaper samples, tissue paper, pipe cleaners, paint/paint-brushes, buttons, "crinkle" paper, etc.)
▲ scissors
▲ stapler

HOW WILL YOU GET HOME TODAY?

Divide a large piece of butcher paper into four equal sections to make a class graph. Color and cut out a car, foot, bicycle, and bus (below), and glue each to the top of a graph section. Title the graph *How Will You Get Home Today?* On the first day of school, discuss transportation to and from school. Reproduce the cutouts below, and have each student color one and cut it out to show how he or she will get home from school. Ask students to write their names on the cutouts. Have students tape their cutouts to the graph. Ask math-related questions about the completed graph, such as *What is the most common way for students to get home from school? What is the least common?* or *How many more (fewer) students walk than ride a bike?* Then use the graph the first week of school as an organizational tool for dismissal.

"EVERYONE'S A STAR" NECKLACE

During first-day introductions, invite students to tell their names and one thing they do well, such as reading, playing baseball, or making cookies. Distribute construction paper stars and have each student draw a picture in the star that shows his or her talent. Have students cut out the stars and punch holes near the top. String the stars onto yarn to make a "teacher necklace" and add a center star "pendant" that says *Mr./Mrs./Ms. _____'s Stars!* Wear the necklace during the first week of school.

"ALL ABOUT ME" BOOKLET

Have each student fold two sheets of photocopy paper in half and staple along the fold to make a blank book. Have students fill the book with the following sentence frames and add accompanying illustrations. Invite students to share their books with a partner during the first week of school. Display the books on students' desks on Back-to-School Night.

page	sentence frame
cover	All About Me by _____
page 1	I go to _____ School.
page 2	My eyes are _____. My hair is _____.
page 3	There are _____ people in my family.
page 4	I like to _____.
page 5	My favorite book is _____.
page 6	One thing I want to learn this year is _____.

SCHOOL HELPER CLASS BOOK

MATERIALS
▲ camera/film
▲ large blank butcher-paper book
▲ crayons or markers

Take the class on a tour of the school. Take photographs of people who help at your school and discuss what they do. "School helpers" could include the principal, custodian, lunch supervisor, secretary, nurse, and music teacher. Tape the photos in a large blank butcher-paper book, one photo per page. Write rhyming sentences for each page such as *(Mrs. Jones) is the principal at our school. We think she is really cool!* (A photo of another helper would be on the next page along with text that follows the pattern of the previous page.)

Mrs. Jones is the principal at our school. We think she is really cool.

Mr. Bob is the custodian at our school. We think he is really cool.

ONE, TWO, OR THREE THINGS ABOUT ME

MATERIALS
▲ basket
▲ small snacks (dried apple slices, teddy bear crackers, fish crackers, etc.)

Have students form a circle on the floor. Pass around a basket of small snacks that represent your classroom September theme or school mascot, such as dried apple slices, teddy bear crackers, or fish crackers. Pass the basket to the first student and invite him or her to choose one, two, or three treats. (Students choose the number of treats that coincides with the number of facts about themselves they want to share.) Before he or she eats each treat, the student tells one thing about himself or herself. Pass the basket until each student has had a chance to share at least one fact.

BURSTING INTO (FIRST) GRADE!

Write a short "welcome back to school" note and reproduce it on 3" (7.5 cm) pieces of paper so each student will receive one. Roll up each note and place it and a small treat inside a deflated balloon. Blow up the balloons with helium, tie them with paper ribbons, and give them to the principal to keep until the end of the day. Just before going home, have the principal deliver the balloons to the door and announce they were mysteriously left in the office with a note to deliver them to your room. Give each student a balloon to take home. When the balloons pop or deflate, students will find out that you sent them a message and will feel welcomed to your class!

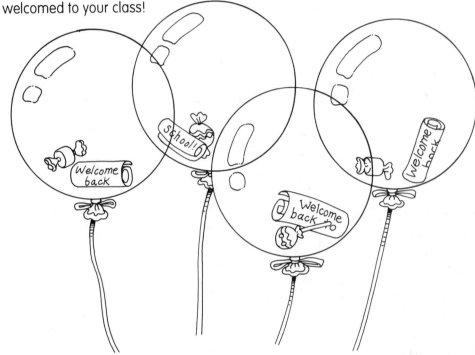

I LIKE SCHOOL! CLASS BOOK

Print the following sentence frames on the chalkboard: *School is cool. I like school. At school, I like to _____.* Have students form a circle near the chalkboard. Invite the class to chant the first two sentences. Have one student read and complete the third sentence. Go around the circle chanting the first two lines and invite each student to complete the third line of the chant. Write each student's sentence on a piece of drawing paper as he or she speaks. Invite students to illustrate their sentences. Compile the pages in a class book titled *I Like School.*

School is cool. I like school.
At school, I like to read books.

"GET TO KNOW THE TEACHER" BOX

Gather personal items that provide information about you (such as photos, books, momentos, or objects from hobbies) and place them in a box. Decorate the box with wrapping paper that represents one of your favorite things and present the box and its contents to the class. Invite students to ask questions so they can learn more about you. Leave the box in a learning center for students to explore. Display the box on Back-to-School Night for parents and children to enjoy.

"IT'S SEPTEMBER" SONG

Teach, and have students practice singing, the following song. Invite students to perform the song for parents on Back-to-School Night.

It's September
(to the tune of "Twinkle, Twinkle, Little Star")

It's September. Fall is here.
It's my favorite time of year.
Boys and girls can make new friends.
Teachers lend a helping hand.
Lots to learn and so much fun.
Back to school for everyone!

PAPER PLATE INTERVIEWS

Divide the class into pairs and provide each pair with a paper plate and crayons or markers. Invite students to trace one of their hands on one side of the paper plate. Then have a student from each pair interview his or her partner and write answers or draw pictures in and around the partner's traced hand. Have partners switch roles and use the other side of the plate to trace a hand and write or draw in and around it. Invite students to refer to the words or drawings on the paper to introduce their partners to the class. Punch holes in the plates and hang them from the ceiling as back-to-school decorations.

LAST-AWHILE NAME TAGS

Have each student use a margarine lid to trace and cut out two circles on white self-adhesive paper. Ask each student to peel off the circles' backing and stick a circle to each side of the lid. Invite each student to draw with permanent marker a self-portrait on one side of the lid. Have students print their names on the other side. Punch two holes in the lid with a hole punch. Invite students to thread yarn through the holes and tie it to make a necklace for wearing the first week of school.

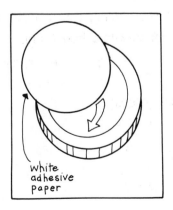

white
adhesive
paper

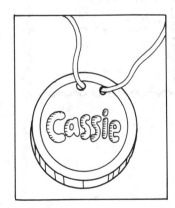

BACK-TO-SCHOOL-NIGHT "DOLLS"

Invite each student to use art supplies to decorate a large paper plate that represents his or her face and hair. Ask each student to tape the plate to a hanger's hook. Just before Back-to-School Night, invite each student to bring in a long-sleeved shirt from home and put it on his or her chair to represent a body. Have students stuff the shirts' arms with newspaper and rest the arms on their desks. Instruct students to insert the "face hangers" into their shirts and tape them to the chairs so the heads are just above the shirts. When parents arrive on Back-to-School Night, have them tour the room and guess which "doll" represents their child.

I AM SPECIAL SACK

HOME ACTIVITY

Take each student's photograph and glue it to a piece of construction paper. Under each photo write *I am (student's name). I am special.* Compile the papers in a class book titled *We are Special.* Place in a canvas bag the class book, an I Am Special Letter, and the book *I Am Special.* Each day in September, send the bag home with a different student. Invite students to return the bag the next day so others can have a chance to take the bag home.

PAPER DOLL

I AM SPECIAL LETTER

Dear Family,

It's a new school year, and I'm making new friends. Everyone in my class is special, just like me! I have brought home an I Am Special Sack to share with you. Please use the sack with me and follow the directions below.

1. Read the book aloud.

2. Discuss with your child why he or she is special.

3. Read the class book to introduce yourself to some other special people in the class.

Enjoy the I Am Special Sack, and please return it tomorrow!

MAKE NEW FRIENDS

The new school year offers teachers and students the perfect chance to make new friends. Help your students develop lasting friendships with the following activities—they're fun, friendly, and fantastic!

LITERATURE LINKS

Arthur's Birthday
by Marc Brown

The Best of Friends
by Josephine Haskell Aldridge

Digby and Kate
by Barbara Baker

Do You Want to Be My Friend?
by Eric Carle

Fast Friends
by James Stevenson

Frog and Toad Are Friends
by Arnold Lobel

Will I Have a Friend?
by Miriam Cohen

CIRCLE OF FRIENDS BULLETIN BOARD

Print the following poem in the center of a butcher-paper circle. Invite each student to trace and cut out two hands from construction paper. Overlap the hands and staple them around the circle's edge. Hang the circle on the bulletin board the first week of school. As September progresses, take photographs of students working and playing together; then hang the photos outside the circle on the bulletin board.

MATERIALS

- ▲ 3'-diameter (91.5 cm-diameter) butcher-paper circle
- ▲ permanent marker
- ▲ stapler
- ▲ construction paper
- ▲ scissors
- ▲ glue
- ▲ camera/film

Circle of Friends
A circle of friendship is right here for you,
With laughter and joy
And lots of fun too.
So take a chance and make a new friend,
And just like a circle, that friendship won't end.

WHERE IS MY NEW FRIEND?

Write each student's name on a blue construction paper rectangle. Hide these name tags around the room. Invite each student to find and pick up one name tag, and help others when he or she is done. Ask each student to read the name on his or her name tag and stand next to that person. Offer help with reading if needed. Invite each student to say *I'd like you to meet _____. He/she is my new friend* to introduce the person whose name he or she chose.

"NEW FRIEND" NECKLACES

Paint dry rigatoni pasta with silver and gold spray paint and set aside. Ask students to write the following poem inside a construction paper circle. *Hi, new friend! How are you? My name is _____. How do you do?* Invite each student to punch two holes in the circle and tie a piece of string to each hole. Ask each student to string the silver and gold pasta on both sides of the circle and tie the strings together to make a necklace. Then ask students to walk around the room and sign the backs of each other's circles as a sign of new friendship. Invite students to wear the necklaces the rest of the day.

Hi, new friend!
How are you?
My name is
Felicia
How do you do?

GOOD MORNING, FRIENDS

Have each student paint a large picture of himself or herself on a piece of construction paper. Write *Good morning to* _____ above each self-portrait. Bind the papers in a class book. To start each day of the first week of school, read the book aloud as a class. Ask each student to reply *Good morning* when his or her page is read. Students will quickly learn each other's names!

THE MORE WE GET TOGETHER

Teach and have students practice the song "The More We Get Together." Then invite students to cut out and paint a Paper Doll Pattern (page 17) to represent themselves. String the dolls on yarn and write one word from the song on each doll so the lyrics can be read from left to right. Hang the string of dolls across the classroom wall.

"I HAVE NEW FRIENDS" GAME

Students will quickly learn about each other with this fun game! Have the class sit on chairs in a circle. Remove one student's chair and ask that student to stand in the circle's center. Have that student say *I have new friends. They _____*. Ask that student to fill in the blank with a specific characteristic such as *have brown hair*, *have a dog*, *love pizza*, or *think math is the best subject.* All students who have that characteristic must jump up and find a new chair. (The chair cannot be next to a student's chair.) At the same time, the student in the center runs to find a chair. The student left without a chair stands in the middle and the game begins again. Play several rounds of the game. For the "grand finale," join the game by standing in the center and saying *I have new friends. They are in Mr./Ms. _____'s class!* Then everyone will have to find a new chair!

HOW TO MAKE FRIENDS CLASS BOOK

Read aloud *Will I Have a Friend?* After story discussion, invite each student to think of one way to make a new friend, such as *Ask a person to play at recess*, *Invite a person to your house for lunch*, or *Choose a person to be your partner in class.* Have each student write his or her sentence on construction paper and illustrate it. Gather the pages in a class book titled *How to Make Friends*.

I invited José to my house for lunch.

FRIENDSHIP FINDER

Provide a Friendship Finder for each student and review each characteristic listed. Ask students to tour the room, show their papers to other students, and try to find a person who fits each category on the Friendship Finder. Ask students to sign their names in the Friendship Finder squares if they find a category to which they belong. Ask students to sit in their seats when they have filled in each square of the Friendship Finder. After 10 to 15 minutes, bring the class together and have them share their findings as you ask questions, such as *Which categories were easiest to complete? Which were hardest?; Did you learn anything new about someone in the class? What?; Which person surprised you the most? Why?; or Do students in our class have a lot in common? What?*

NEW FRIENDS SONG

Teach and have students practice the following song by singing it together first and then by singing in a "round." Invite students to perform the song for parents at Back-to-School Night.

New Friends

(to the tune of "Are You Sleeping?")

It's September.
It's September.
Fall is near.
Fall is near.
We are making new friends.
We are making new friends.
School is here.
School is here.

FRIENDSHIP FINDER

likes spinach	has more than 3 brothers or sisters	has been to another state	has green eyes
likes snakes	has ridden a horse	can hop on one foot ten times	collects something
has seen real dinosaur bones	can do five jumping jacks	knows the name of the capital of his or her state	is wearing white shoes

September © 1997 Creative Teaching Press

COOL SCHOOL RULES

The school year is always easier when you start with some "cool school rules." Make following directions and learning the "rules of the room" fun with these practical ideas. They're sure to get your students started on the right track.

LITERATURE LINKS

Miss Nelson Is Missing
by Harry Allard

Never Spit on Your Shoes
by Denys Cazet

Norma Jean, Jumping Bean
by Joanna Cole

Starting School
by Janet Ahlberg

This Is the Way We Go to School
by Edith Baer

"PICK AN APPLE" JOB BOARD

Twist brown butcher paper to form a large tree trunk and branches. Staple the tree to a bulletin board. Attach calendar-cutout leaves to the tree. Laminate calendar-cutout apples, one for each student. (Precut apple and leaf shapes are available at teacher-supply stores.) Write a different "classroom helper" job on 10 of the apples. Jobs could include paper passer, line leader, chalkboard cleaner, or paper collector. Pin all the apples on the tree so the writing does not show. Invite students to come to the board and choose an apple. Students who choose "job apples" have that job for a week. Students who choose blank apples do not have jobs. Have students choose apples again the next week. If a student chooses a job apple a second time, invite him or her to give the job apple to a student with a blank one. Continue this method of choosing jobs throughout the month of September so each student has a chance to do at least one job.

MATERIALS
▲ brown butcher paper
▲ scissors
▲ stapler
▲ calendar-cutout leaves
▲ calendar-cutout apples
▲ pushpins

CLASS CONSTITUTION

Have students brainstorm a list of positive rules for the classroom, such as *Keep hands, feet, and objects to yourself; Respect the rights and feelings of others;* and *Listen.* Invite the class to vote for the five or six most important rules for a successful classroom. Write the rules on a large sheet of tan butcher paper. Tear around the edges of the paper and wrinkle the paper so it looks old and worn. Write *Class Constitution* at the top of the paper. Ask students to "take an oath" to follow the Class Constitution, and invite them to sign the bottom. Hang the Class Constitution for all to see and remember.

MATERIALS

▲ large sheet of tan butcher paper
▲ permanent markers

Class Constitution

1. Keep hands, feet, and objects to yourself.

2. Respect the rights and feelings of others.

3. Listen.

4. Use "inside voices."

5. Share.

Paul David Jacob Cara Mia Joel Leslie Shelby Chelsey Brent

BE A BETTER BUS RIDER!

MATERIALS

▲ Bus Pattern (page 29)
▲ crayons or markers
▲ scissors
▲ photocopies of last year's student photos (one for each student)
▲ stapler

The first week of school, invite a bus driver to visit your class and discuss bus safety. After the visit, discuss rules for riding the bus, such as *Sit quietly, Do not disturb the driver,* and *Keep your hands and head inside the bus.* Invite students to write three bus rules on a Bus Pattern. Have students color and cut out the patterns. Ask students to glue a photocopy of last year's school photo in a bus window. Staple the buses on a bulletin board titled *Be a Better Bus Rider!*

1. Sit quietly.
2. Do not disturb the driver.
3. Keep your hands and head inside.

RULE JAR

MATERIALS
▲ slips of paper
▲ jar

Write role-playing directions for classroom rules and procedures on separate slips of paper, one slip for each student. Role-playing directions could include *Show how to carry scissors*, *Show how to sit on the floor*, or *Show where to place your math papers*. Include a few "how not to" directions, such as *Show how NOT to listen*, *Show how NOT to line up* or *Show how NOT to sit in your chair*. Place the directions in a jar labeled *Rule Jar*. Invite each student to choose a slip of paper from the jar and perform its directions. Use the jar two or three times during the first week of school so students can learn rules and procedures in a fun way!

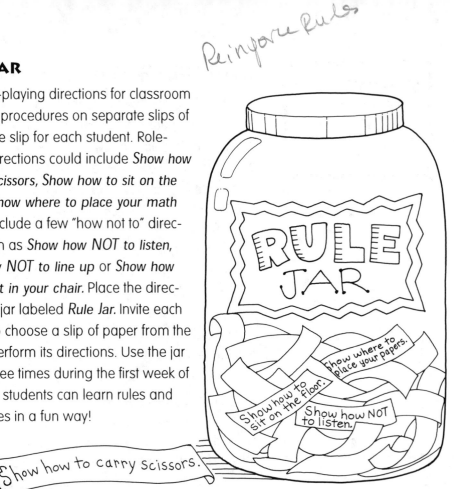

PLAYGROUND TOUR

MATERIALS
▲ playground equipment

Divide the class into groups, one group for each piece of playground equipment on your playground. Meet with each group, and help the members make up a "routine" that demonstrates the proper use of the equipment. Have students design narration for their routine that includes a list of equipment "do's and don'ts." Invite each group to practice the routine by performing it for the rest of the class. For the "real performance," send groups to their piece of equipment to perform their routines for visiting classes that rotate from one piece of equipment to another.

NEVER SPIT ON YOUR SHOES CLASS BOOK

Read aloud *Never Spit on Your Shoes*. Invite students to pretend they are characters from the book and think of other silly, but relevant, school rules such as *Never eat your math paper* or *Wear clothes to school every day*. Invite each student to choose a silly rule to illustrate on construction paper. Have students write the rules above the illustrations. Bind the papers in a class book titled *Never Spit on Your Shoes and Other Silly School Rules*.

SCHOOL YEAR CONTRACT

HOME ACTIVITY

Write your classroom rules on the lines provided on the School Year Contract before photocopying a contract for each student. Invite students to bring home a contract, complete it with their families, and return the contract within a week. Keep the contracts in a file and refer to them when meeting with students or parents throughout the year.

SCHOOL YEAR CONTRACT

Dear Family,

Welcome to a new school year! To keep the classroom a fun, happy, and safe place to learn, some classroom rules have been established. Please read and discuss the rules with your child and then sign the contract below.

1. _____

2. _____

3. _____

4. _____

5. _____

6. _____

BUS

1.
2.
3.

SCHOOL YEAR CONTRACT

Dear Family,

Welcome to a new school year! To keep the classroom a fun, happy, and safe place to learn, some classroom rules have been established. Please read and discuss the rules with your child and then sign the contract below.

1. _____

2. _____

3. _____

4. _____

5. _____

6. _____

I have read and understand the classroom rules. I will do my best to follow the rules this year.

_____
student signature

I have read the classroom rules with my child. I understand that my child is responsible for following these rules this school year.

_____
parent signature

September © 1998 Creative Teaching Press

APPLES

It's September and that means apple season! Add some of this delicious fall fruit to your curriculum by "picking" a few of the following apple activities— they're yummy!

LITERATURE LINKS

Apples and More Apples
by Michael K. Smith

The Apple Pie Family
by Cary Thompson

The Apple Pie Tree
by Zoe Hall

Apple Tree
by Barrie Watts

The Seasons of Arnold's Apple Tree
by Gail Gibbons

Ten Apples up on Top
by Theodore LeSieg

"AN APPLE WITH CLASS" BULLETIN BOARD

Cut two large identical apple shapes from white butcher paper. Staple one of the apples in the center of a bulletin board. Title the bulletin board *An Apple with Class.* Cut the other apple into puzzle pieces, one for each student and one for yourself. Number the back of the pieces as you cut each piece. Use red marker to outline the edges of each puzzle piece so each piece stands out when the puzzle is put together. Ask students to decorate a puzzle piece with their name and pictures or words that represent hobbies, favorite animals or school subjects, or other unique characteristics. Have students gather around the bulletin board. Beginning with the student who has puzzle piece #1, have each student share his or her piece and staple it onto the bulletin-board apple. Continue sharing until the apple puzzle is complete.

MATERIALS
- ▲ white butcher paper
- ▲ red permanent marker
- ▲ crayons or markers
- ▲ stapler
- ▲ scissors

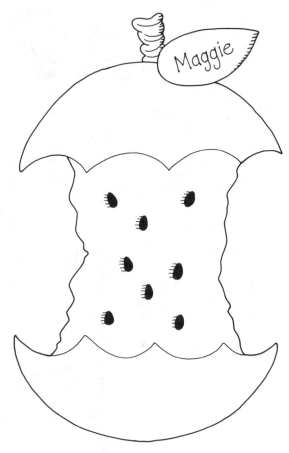

EATEN-APPLE ART

Have each student tear along the "long sides" of a piece of 8 1/2" x 11" (21.5 cm x 28 cm) white paper to create the "white part" of an eaten apple. Then ask each student to fold a 9" x 12" (23 cm x 30.5 cm) piece of red construction paper in half. Have students draw a large umbrella shape on the red paper. Have students cut through both halves of the paper to create two identical umbrella shapes. Ask students to glue one umbrella shape, points facing down, to the top of the torn paper to represent the top of the eaten apple. Instruct students to glue the other umbrella shape, points facing up, to the bottom of the torn paper for the apple bottom. Have students twist a brown paper strip into a "stem" and cut a leaf from green paper. Invite students to glue the stem and leaf to the apple top. Have students glue real apple seeds in the apple's center. Hang the apples in the hall or class for all to admire.

MATERIALS
- ▲ 8 1/2" x 11" (21.5 cm x 28 cm) white paper
- ▲ 9" x 12" (23 cm x 30.5 cm) piece of red construction paper
- ▲ brown paper strips
- ▲ 2" x 4" (5 cm x 10 cm) brown paper strips
- ▲ green construction paper
- ▲ real apple seeds
- ▲ scissors
- ▲ glue

APPLE SMILES

Explain that an apple is sometimes called *nature's toothbrush* because eating apples helps clean your teeth when you do not have a toothbrush with you. For a fun reminder, first have each student spread peanut butter on two apple slices. Ask students to place four miniature marshmallows on one apple slice near the skin to represent teeth. Invite students to gently press one apple slice on top of the other, peanut butter sides together, to make a "mouth" with clean, white "teeth." Then invite students to eat their "apple smiles."

MATERIALS
- ▲ 1/2"-thick (1 cm-thick) red apple slices
- ▲ peanut butter
- ▲ large bag of miniature marshmallows
- ▲ plastic knives

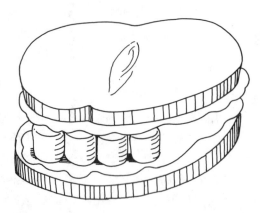

SOLAR COOKING WITH APPLES

MATERIALS
- ▲ "apple book" (see Literature Links, page 31)
- ▲ Styrofoam cups
- ▲ aluminum foil
- ▲ peeled apple slices
- ▲ sugar
- ▲ cinnamon

Complete this activity on a warm, sunny morning in the beginning of September. Read aloud and discuss an "apple book." Have students predict what would happen if apples were placed in the hot sun for a long period of time. To test predictions, have each student line the inside of a Styrofoam cup with aluminum foil. Next, have each child place two or three peeled apple slices inside the cup. Ask students to sprinkle approximately 1/2 teaspoon sugar and 1/4 teaspoon cinnamon over the apples. Invite students to place their cups outside in the sun until the apples are soft and warm; then have students eat and enjoy!

WAY UP HIGH POCKET-CHART POEM

MATERIALS
- ▲ sentence strips
- ▲ pocket chart

Write the following poem on sentence strips and place them in a pocket chart. Teach, and have students practice reciting and acting out, the poem. Invite students to perform the poem for other classes or for parents on Back-to-School Night.

Way up High	**Motions**
Way up high in an apple tree,	*Students wave hands overhead.*
Two little apples smiled at me.	*Students point to smile on face.*
I shook that tree as hard as I could,	*Students shake hands around "trunk."*
And down came the apples.	*Students move hands down.*
Mmmm . . . they were good!	*Students rub stomach.*

APPLES-UP-ON-TOP MATH

MATERIALS
- ▲ large, dry white beans
- ▲ *Ten Apples up on Top* by Theodore LeSieg
- ▲ red spray paint
- ▲ plastic animals

In advance, make "apple manipulatives" by painting large, dry white beans with red spray paint. Read aloud and discuss *Ten Apples up on Top*. Divide the class into pairs and provide each pair with 10 to 20 apple manipulatives and two or three plastic animals. Invite partners to take turns and create math stories for their partners to solve from apple manipulatives and plastic animals. For example, a student might arrange "apples" and a plastic cat and dog and say *Cat had three apples up on top. Dog had two apples up on top. How many did they have altogether?* Have each partner take several turns. Then make the class book described below.

> Cat had three apples up on top.

APPLES-UP-ON-TOP CLASS BOOKS

MATERIALS
- ▲ slips of paper
- ▲ *Ten Apples up on Top* by Theodore LeSieg
- ▲ 8 1/2" x 11" (21.5 cm x 28 cm) white construction paper
- ▲ crayons or markers
- ▲ red construction paper
- ▲ scissors
- ▲ glue
- ▲ bookbinding materials

In advance, write the numbers one through ten on individual slips of paper several times so each student can have a number. Read aloud *Ten Apples up on Top*. Invite each student to draw on white construction paper a picture of himself or herself. Have each student choose a number from a hat and cut out that number of small apples from red construction paper. Ask students to glue the apples on top of the heads on their drawings. Invite students to complete the sentence frame: *(number) apples on top of (student's name)*. Bind ten papers in number order to make three or more class books; then share the books with the class.

Lucy

Three apples on top of Lucy.

APPLE PRINT BULLETIN BOARD BORDERS

MATERIALS

▲ several large apple halves

▲ red, green, and yellow tempera paint

▲ paper plates (to hold paint)

▲ sentence strips

Create delightful borders for your September bulletin boards with this easy patterning/art activity. Divide the class into groups. Invite each group to dip several large apple halves into red, green, and yellow tempera paint and stamp the halves in a pattern on sentence strips. (All groups can create the same pattern or you can assign a different pattern to each group.) Have groups use markers to label each apple and show the pattern. For example, students might write *red, green, yellow; red, green, yellow* under the apple prints. Hang strips of the same pattern around each bulletin board as a border.

APPLE MINI-BOOKS

MATERIALS

▲ 5 1/2" x 8 1/2" (14 cm x 21.5 cm) white drawing paper

▲ 8 1/2" x 11" (21.5 cm x 28 cm) construction paper

▲ stapler

▲ crayons or markers

To make a mini-book, invite each student to staple four 5 1/2" x 8 1/2" (14 cm x 21.5 cm) pieces of white drawing paper inside a piece of 8 1/2" x 11" (21.5 cm x 28 cm) construction paper that has been folded in half. Ask each student to number the book's pages and write the following phrases on each page:

page	phrase
page 1 (title page)	*Apples* by (student's name)
page 2	Dedicated to (name)
page 3	Apples in juice.
page 4	Apples in a tree.
page 5	Apples in sauce.
page 6	Apples for free!
page 7	Apples in a pie.
page 8	Apples in me!

Invite students to illustrate each page, design a cover, and title the book *Apples.* Have students share their books; then display them on Back-to-School Night.

APPLE EXPERIMENT

Invite students to predict which special ingredient (lemon juice, grape juice, or water) best keeps apples from decaying and turning brown. Divide the class into groups of four. Provide each group with four Recording Sheets, four apple slices, four large plastic cups, and four paper towel sheets. Invite students to record their initial predictions on the recording sheet. Go around to each group and pour lemon juice into one cup, grape juice into a second cup, and water into a third. Ask groups to dip a different apple slice in each cup, remove the slices, and place them on the paper towels. (Students do not dip the fourth apple slice.) Have groups set the apple slices aside, check the apples from time to time, and record what they see and the order in which the apples turn brown. As a class, compare and discuss group observations and predictions.

SEED PREDICTION

Have the class gather around a large numbered floor graph with the labels *Number of Students* and *Number of Seeds* (see illustration). Explain that most apples have from 0 to 15 seeds, and invite each student to predict how many seeds will be in an apple you display. Invite each student to come to the floor graph and lay a white bean on the graph to show his or her prediction. As a class, count the number of students who made each prediction. Cut open the apple and count the seeds. Compare the results to the predictions on the graph.

Number of seeds

Number of students

0 1 2 3 4 5 6 7 8 9 10 11 12 13 14 15

How many seeds will the apple have?

MATERIALS

▲ apple slices
▲ toothpicks
▲ miniature marshmallows
▲ gumdrops
▲ dried apricots
▲ raisins
▲ peanut butter
▲ banana slices
▲ olives
▲ carrot slices
▲ celery
▲ plastic knives

APPLE CRITTERS

Invite each student to use an apple slice, the foods described in the materials list, several toothpicks, and a plastic knife to create an Apple Critter (an "edible animal" based on a real or imaginary creature). Take a photograph of each Apple Critter before inviting students to eat. Glue each photo to a piece of construction paper, and invite students to write their names and the critter's name on their paper. Bind the papers into a class recipe book titled *Apple Critters.*

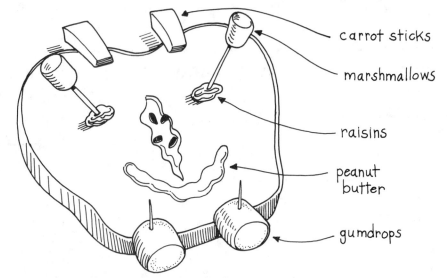

carrot sticks

marshmallows

raisins

peanut butter

gumdrops

MATERIALS

▲ Applesauce Recipe (page 39)

CROCK-POT APPLESAUCE

Send home with each student the recipe on page 39. Invite students to make the Applesauce Recipe with their families and return the "jar journal" (the bottom portion of the recipe) within one week. Bind the jar journals in a class book titled *What's inside the Applesauce Jar?*

RECORDING SHEET

_____'s Apple Experiment

I predict _____ will keep the apple from turning brown the best.

Ingredient	What I Saw	The Order in Which the Apples Turned Brown (First, Second, Third, Last)
lemon juice		
water		
grape juice		
nothing		

The apple with _____ on it was the last to turn brown.

September © 1998 Creative Teaching Press

APPLESAUCE RECIPE

Dear Family,

This fall we are using apples to help us learn new things. You can use apples and make applesauce with me to help me learn about counting, measuring, and fractions. Please make the recipe with me by _____, and help me complete the "jar journal." We'll have a delicious time!

1. Peel and slice five apples. Place the apples in a large mixing bowl.
2. Mix in 2.5 tablespoons honey.
3. Add 1 teaspoon cinnamon.
4. Cook in a covered pan or Crock-pot until soft.
5. Stir, cool, and enjoy!
6. Complete the jar journal and return it by _____.

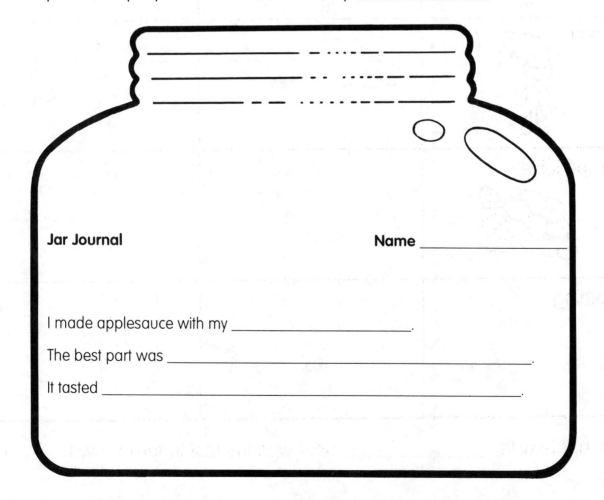

Jar Journal   **Name** _____

I made applesauce with my _____.

The best part was _____.

It tasted _____.

FALL LEAVES

In many places in North America, the change from summer to autumn brings falling temperatures and falling leaves! Help your students welcome autumn by having them complete the following leaf activities. Your students will "fall" for them!

LITERATURE LINKS

I See Colors
by Rozanne Lanczak Williams (CTP)

Johnny Maple-Leaf
by Alvon R. Tresselt

Look at Leaves
by Rena K. Kirkpatrick

Marmalade's Yellow Leaf
by Cindy Wheeler

Patterns of Nature
by Jeffrey J. Baler

Red Leaf, Yellow Leaf
by Lois Ehlert

What Happens in the Autumn?
by Suzanne Venino

FALLING LEAVES BULLETIN BOARD

Have students brainstorm "autumn words," such as *fall*, *rake*, *football*, *chilly*, *harvest*, and *windy*. Invite each student to choose a different word and write it in the center of a Leaf Pattern. Ask each student to cut out his or her leaf and spread glue over it, leaving space around the word. Have students choose a dry red food (such as paprika), a dry brown food (such as crushed Corn Flakes or cinnamon), a dry green food (such as basil), or a dry yellow food (such as cornmeal) and sprinkle it on their leaves. Have students shake off the excess "sprinkles" and staple their leaves to a bulletin board titled *We're Falling for Fall Words!* Have students use the words throughout September and October for creative-writing activities.

MATERIALS
▲ Leaf Pattern (page 45)
▲ glue
▲ scissors
▲ dried foods in various fall colors

READ A LEAF

MATERIALS

▲ large tree branch
▲ bucket of clay or sand
▲ construction paper leaves
▲ laminator
▲ paper clips
▲ small bushel basket

Push a large tree branch into a bucket of clay or sand. Print each student's name on a laminated construction paper leaf (pre-cut leaves are available at teacher-supply stores) and insert an "unfolded" s-shaped paper clip into each leaf. Place the leaves in a bushel basket near the "tree." Each morning, as students arrive, have them remove their leaf from the basket and hang it on the tree. When taking attendance, look at the leaves left in the basket and note which students are absent. At the end of the day, use the leaves for dismissal. Choose one leaf from the tree, read the name on it aloud, and drop it in the basket. As that student's name is called, he or she is invited to choose a second leaf, read it, drop it in the basket, and line up at the door. Have students continue choosing and reading leaves until the class has lined up. In this way, the leaves will be returned to the basket and ready for the next day!

LEAF MAGNETS OR PINS

MATERIALS

▲ colorful fall leaves
▲ paper towel
▲ newspaper
▲ heavy books
▲ paint pens, acrylic paints, or permanent markers
▲ nontoxic varnish
▲ pin backs (available at craft stores)
▲ self-sticking magnets (available at craft stores)

Have each student collect a colorful fall leaf. Ask students to spread the leaves between paper towels or newspaper. Place heavy books on top and let the leaves dry for about a week. Invite each student to make designs on his or her leaf with paint pens, acrylic paints, or permanent markers. After school, paint the dry leaves with several coats of nontoxic varnish. Cover one side at a time, allowing the varnish to dry between coats. The next day, invite each student to attach to the leaf backs either a pin back or two self-sticking magnets. Invite students to bring the leaves home and present them to their families as gifts.

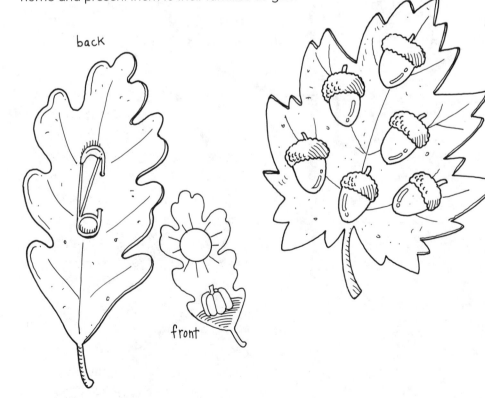

back

front

LEAFY CROWNS

MATERIALS
- ▲ "The Leaf Dance" (below)
- ▲ sentence strips
- ▲ leaves brought from home
- ▲ glue
- ▲ stapler

Give each student a "Leaf Poem" and have him or her glue it to the center of a sentence strip. Practice the poem until the class can recite it. Then invite each student to sort by color, size, and shape several leaves he or she brought from home. Have each student glue his or her leaves on the sentence strip (on either side of the poem) to show a color, size, or shape pattern. Fit the sentence strips to the students' heads and staple them to make crowns. Have students wear their crowns and perform the poem for other classes or for parents on Back-to-School Night.

The Leaf Dance

Red and yellow, green and brown,
Orange and rust and tan.
I can do the leaf dance,
The leaf dance, yes I can!

I am floating to the ground.
The air is like a fan.
I can do the leaf dance,
The leaf dance, yes I can!

The Leaf Dance

Red and yellow, green and brown,
Orange and rust and tan.
I can do the leaf dance,
The leaf dance, yes I can!

I am floating to the ground.
The air is like a fan.
I can do the leaf dance,
The leaf dance, yes I can!

THE LEAVES ARE FALLING

Teach, and have students practice, the following song. Invite students to perform the song for other classes or for parents on Back-to-School Night.

MATERIALS
▲ none

The Leaves Are Falling
(to the tune of "The Ants Go Marching")

Motions

The leaves are falling one by one,   *Students wave one finger.*
Hurrah, hurrah!
The leaves are falling one by one,
Hurrah, hurrah!
The leaves are falling one by one.
A red one lands upon my thumb.   *Students push palm on thumb.*
And they all go falling   *Students wiggle fingers down.*
Down to the ground, to be   *Students make raking motions.*
Raked by me.
Boom, boom, boom.

Other verses
The leaves are falling two by two.   *Students wave two fingers.*
An orange one lands upon my shoe.   *Students point to shoe.*

The leaves are falling three by three.   *Students wave three fingers.*
A rust one falls upon my knee.   *Students point to knee.*

The leaves are falling four by four.   *Students wave four fingers.*
I won't be raking anymore!   *Students shake heads.*
And they all go falling   *Students wiggle fingers down.*
Down to the ground, to be   *Students shake heads.*
Raked up no more!

Fall Leaves

43

HOME ACTIVITY

FALL LEAF COLLECTION

Send home the following Parent Letter with each student. Invite students to follow the letter's directions and create a fall leaf collection. Display the leaf collections next to magnifying glasses or microscopes as a learning center.

Dear Family,

We are celebrating fall by working with leaves. Please follow the directions below and help me make a leaf collection. The collection needs to be sent to school by _____ so I can share it with my friends.

1. Take a walk and find as many kinds of the following leaves as you can.
   - tree "needles"
   - long leaves
   - "zigzag-edged" leaves
   - round leaves
   - pointy leaves
   - colorful leaves

2. Press the leaves between paper towels or newspaper. Lay heavy books over the leaves. Keep the leaves covered for one week.

3. After the leaves have dried, tape each leaf to a piece of paper. Label each leaf with its category name.

4. Bind the papers in a notebook or paper cover.

5. Write *Leaf Collection* on the cover and decorate it.

LEAF PATTERN

NATIONAL LITERACY MONTH

It's the beginning of a new school year, the perfect time to celebrate National Literacy Month! The following activities will help your students understand the importance of reading. And when they are completed, your students will quickly see that they need to "read to succeed"!

LITERATURE LINKS

I Can Read
by Rozanne Lanczak Williams
(CTP)

I Can Read with My Eyes Shut
by Dr. Seuss

I Like Books
by Anthony Browne

More than Anything
by Marie Bradby

Reading
by Jan Ormerod

When Will I Read?
by Miriam Cohen

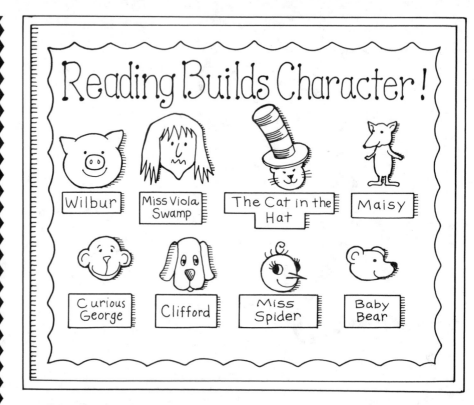

Reading Builds Character!

Wilbur · Miss Viola Swamp · The Cat in the Hat · Maisy · Curious George · Clifford · Miss Spider · Baby Bear

READING BUILDS CHARACTER BULLETIN BOARD

Have each student draw and cut out a main character from a favorite book. Invite each student to introduce and describe his or her character and favorite book, and then staple the character to a bulletin board titled *Reading Builds Character.* The next day, display several of the described books near the bulletin board and invite students to read them.

MATERIALS
▲ construction paper
▲ crayons or markers
▲ scissors
▲ stapler
▲ several books

MATERIALS

▲ magazines
▲ scissors
▲ glue
▲ 2" x 6" (5 cm x 15 cm) construction-paper strip
▲ crayons or markers
▲ laminator

TALKING BOOKMARKS

Invite each student to cut out a person's face from a magazine and glue it to the center of a 2" x 6" (5 cm x 15 cm) construction-paper strip to make a bookmark. Ask students to draw a "speech bubble" above the mouth. Have students write a reading slogan such as *Reading makes me smile* or *Reading helps me get "ahead"* in the speech bubble. Laminate the bookmarks and invite students to trade them with partners in celebration of National Literacy Month.

MATERIALS

▲ books

READ WITH A FRIEND DAY

Designate one day of the week (during the month of September) to be Read with a Friend Day. On this special day, have student partners choose a book and read it together for 10 to 15 minutes. Then invite partners to share with the class what they read.

MATERIALS

▲ chalkboard and chalk
▲ four picture books
▲ slips of paper

MYSTERY READER

To celebrate National Literacy Month, choose a "mystery reader" to visit your classroom and read a book to the class. (The mystery reader could be the principal, the school nurse, a community leader, or the physical education teacher.) To begin, choose four picture books, number the books from one to four, and rest them on the chalk rail. Invite each student to guess which book will be read by the mystery reader. Leave the books on the rail. On the designated day, invite the mystery reader to enter the room and choose the book he or she will read to the class. Have the mystery reader share the book and discuss it with the class.

MATERIALS

▲ *I Can Read* by Rozanne Lanczak Williams (CTP)
▲ backpack
▲ blank notebook
▲ Backpack Parent Letter (page 49)

READING BACKPACK

HOME ACTIVITY

Place *I Can Read* in a backpack with a blank notebook and a Backpack Parent Letter. Send the backpack home with a different student each night in September. Share a child's notebook entry each morning after the backpack is returned. Display the notebook at Open House or on Back-to-School Night for families to enjoy.

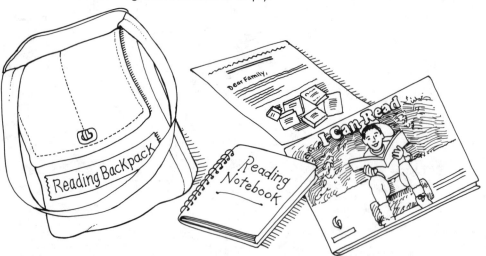

BACKPACK PARENT LETTER

Dear Family,

It's National Literacy Month, and we're celebrating! Please help me complete the following task to celebrate reading. We'll have a terrific time!

1. Read the book together.

2. Talk about the story.

3. Write on a blank page in the notebook what you liked about the book. (We'll be reading your entry aloud tomorrow.)

Please return the backpack tomorrow so another student can discover the joy of reading with his or her family!

LABOR DAY

Since 1930, every state in the United States has celebrated Labor Day to show appreciation for the country's workers. The following Labor Day activities will help your students think about the importance of hard work and setting goals for a future career. The activities are so much fun, students won't want to stop "working"!

LITERATURE LINKS

Both My Parents Work
by Katherine Leiner

Labor Day
by Geoffrey Scott

100 Words About Working
by Richard Brown

People Working
by Douglas Florian

If I Could Work
by Terence Blacker

When I Grow Up
by Heidi Goennel

LABOR-SAVING INVENTIONS BULLETIN BOARD

Have students brainstorm labor-saving inventions for the home, such as a dishwasher, a clothes washer and dryer, and a vacuum cleaner. Then have students think of their own imaginary labor-saving inventions, such as a homework machine or a chocolate-milk maker. Invite students to illustrate their inventions and label important invention parts. Have students write the invention names above the illustrations. Hang the illustrations on a bulletin board titled *We'll Take the Labor out of Your Day!*

MATERIALS
▲ 12" x 18" (30.5 cm x 46 cm) construction paper
▲ crayon or markers
▲ stapler

CAREERS FROM A TO Z

Discuss Labor Day and careers. Have each student choose a different bulletin board letter from a hat. Ask students to think of a career whose name begins with their letter, such as *A* for astronaut, *B* for baker, and *C* for computer programmer. Invite each student to glue his or her letter to a piece of construction paper, write the career name using the letter, and illustrate the career. Bind the papers in a class book titled *Careers from A to Z.*

WHAT DO YOU DO? INTERVIEW

Have students take home an Interview Form and interview an adult about his or her career. Ask students to return the form the next day. Invite each student to share the form and tell what he or she learned from the interview.

INTERVIEW FORM

Name _____

1. What is your name?_____

2. What is your job title?_____

3. How long have you been doing this job?_____

4. What do you do at work? Name three things.

_____

_____

_____

5. What do you like about your job?_____

6. What don't you like about your job?_____

7. What did you have to learn to do your job? _____

_____

8. Would this be a good job for me? _____ Why or why not?_____

_____

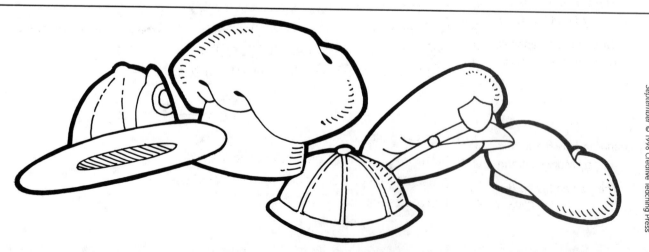

September © 1998 Creative Teaching Press

GRANDPARENTS' DAY

First Sunday after Labor Day

There is something special about the relationship between grandparent and grandchild. Help your students share their love for grandparents and older friends by celebrating Grandparents' Day. The following activities will get you started.

LITERATURE LINKS

At Grammy's House
by Eve Rice

Cornrows
by Camille Yarborough

The Grandma Mix-Up
by Emily Arnold McCully

Grandma's Scrapbook
by Josephine Nobisso

I Have Four Names for My Grandfather
by Kathryn Lasky

My Grandma Has Black Hair
by Mary Hoffman

The Remembering Box
by Eth Clifford

SCENTED GRANDPARENTS' DAY CARDS

Invite each student to cut out and color a Grandparents' Day Card. Have students insert the following words in order: *you, say, you, Grandparents' Day* to complete the poem on the inside of the reproducible. Ask students to trace the heart on the card with glue. Invite students to sprinkle flavored gelatin on the heart and then shake off the powder. Punch two holes on the left side of the dried cards. Have students string a ribbon through the holes and tie a bow. Send the scented cards home for students to give, or invite students to present them at a Grandparents' Day celebration (page 54).

MATERIALS

▲ Grandparents' Day Card (page 55)
▲ flavored gelatin
▲ scissors
▲ crayons
▲ glue

MATERIALS

▲ Celebration Invitations (page 56)
▲ games such as Bingo
▲ songs such as "The Leaves Are Falling" (page 43)
▲ art project such as Milk Carton Birdhouses (page 59)
▲ punch and cookies
▲ cups and napkins
▲ small gift such as a Grandparents' Day Card (page 53)

MATERIALS

▲ *The Remembering Box* by Eth Clifford
▲ index cards
▲ small boxes with lids
▲ wrapping paper
▲ tape

GRANDPARENTS' DAY CELEBRATION

The week before Grandparents' Day, send a completed Celebration Invitation home with each student. Students should escort their guests to school on celebration day and participate in a variety of activities such as games, songs, and art projects. Serve punch and cookies as each student presents his or her grandparent or older friend with a small gift.

REMEMBERING BOX

Read aloud and discuss *The Remembering Box*. Invite students to write a poem on an index card about an object they would like to keep in a "remembering box" as a reminder of a grandparent or older friend. Have students use the following format to write the poem.

Format
Object Name
Two words describing the object
Where the object can be found
What the object is used for
Other words for the object

Example
Grandma's quilt
Old, tattered
On the edge of my bed
Keeps me safe and warm
Special blanket

Invite each student to wrap a box with a lid with wrapping paper. (Be sure the box is large enough to hold an index card). Have students wrap the box bottom and top separately so the lid can be removed. Ask each student to tape his or her poem in the inside bottom of the box, place the lid on top, and present the box to a grandparent or older friend on Grandparents' Day.

GRANDPARENTS' DAY CARD

I really want to tell _____

I really want to _____

I'm so glad to wish _____

Happy _____!

CELEBRATION INVITATION

Dear Grandparent or Older Friend,

You are cordially invited to a Grandparents' Day Celebration on

_____ from _____ to _____.

The celebration will be held at _____

_____.

Please join us for a day of fun and surprises! See you there!

- -

RSVP

I (we) will be happy to be the guest of _____
                                                                        student's name

for the Grandparents' Day Celebration!

Visitor name(s): _____.

September © 1998 Creative Teaching Press

GRANDMA MOSES' BIRTHDAY

September 7

Grandma Moses got her name because she began painting at the age of 77. She used bright, rich colors to paint from memory pictures of American rural life. Celebrate this famous painter's birthday with the following activities; they'll bring out the artist in every student!

LITERATURE LINKS

Grandma Moses
by Nancy Tompkins

Grandma Moses: Painter of Rural America
by Zibby O'Neal

Grandma Moses' Night Before Christmas
by Clement C. Moore

Grandma Moses: The Grand Old Lady of American Art
by Martha Laing

Inspirations: Stories about Women Artists
by Leslie Sills

Shelby

SEPTEMBER SUNSETS

Invite each student to use red, orange, and yellow watercolors to paint thick horizontal stripes that cover an entire sheet of white construction paper. Have students go over the stripes with water on a paintbrush until the stripes become muted and resemble an autumn sky at dusk. Invite each student to use black tempera paint and paint a silhouette of a country scene over the "sky." Students can paint trees, fences, cornstalks, scarecrows, barns, or any other country object. Display the paintings on a bulletin board titled *September Sunsets*.

MATERIALS

▲ red, orange, and yellow watercolors
▲ paintbrushes
▲ 8 1/2" x 11" (21.5 cm x 28 cm) white construction paper
▲ black tempera paint

PAINTING FROM MEMORY

MATERIALS
▲ tempera paints/paint-brushes
▲ 8 1/2" x 11" (21.5 cm x 28 cm) white construction paper

Explain that Grandma Moses painted scenes from memory. Invite each student to think of a favorite September event, such as the first day of school or a Labor Day picnic. Ask students to close their eyes and imagine the event. Ask questions such as *What do you see?; What do you hear?;* and *What do you smell?* Invite students to open their eyes and paint a picture of the event from memory. Ask students to add details to their paintings so others can guess the event by simply observing the drawings. Invite each student to share his or her painting with the class. Display the paintings for all to admire.

BARNYARD BRAINSTORMS

MATERIALS
▲ tempera paint/paint-brushes
▲ 12" x 18" (30.5 cm x 46 cm) white construction paper
▲ Styrofoam packing peanuts
▲ glue
▲ crayons or markers
▲ scissors

Explain that Grandma Moses liked to paint rural scenes. Have the class brainstorm several country objects, such as a tractor, a barn, a farmhouse, farm animals, a gravel road, or ponds and lakes. Invite each student to choose three objects from the list that he or she would like to show in a country scene. Have each student paint pictures of the country objects, cut them out, and set them aside. Invite students to draw and color a background for the objects. Have each student glue Styrofoam packing peanuts on the backs of his or her cutouts and glue the cutouts to the background. (The raised cutouts give a three-dimensional effect to the scenes.) Display the scenes near the heading *Barnyard Brainstorms.*

NATURE DAY

Greenpeace was founded on September 15, 1971 as an organization committed to a "green and peaceful world." Help your students appreciate the wonders of the earth with the following Nature Day activities. They're fun, "naturally"!

LITERATURE LINKS

The Berenstain Bears Don't Pollute Anymore
by Stan Berenstain

The Forgotten Forest
by Laurence Anholt

How Green Are You?
by David Bellamy

Recycle!
by Gail Gibbons

World Water Watch
by Michelle Koch

MILK CARTON BIRDHOUSES

Have each student bring in a clean half-gallon milk carton. Invite students to pry open the carton top, cover the carton with construction paper, and decorate it with crayons or markers. Cover the cartons with clear self-adhesive paper to protect the construction paper. Show students how to use scissors to cut a hole about the size of a doorknob in one side of the carton, about 2" (5 cm) below where the top folds. Help students make two small holes with a nail in the other side of the carton. (The top hole should be about 1/3 from the top. The bottom hole should be lined up with the top one and be about 1/3 up from the bottom.) Have students lace approximately 2' (61 cm) of string through the top nail hole, along the inside of the carton, and out the bottom hole. Invite students to make a bed for the birds by laying dried grass in the carton bottom. Ask students to close the top of the carton and seal it with clear packing tape. Invite students to go home and hang the birdhouses by wrapping the string's ends around two nails that have been hammered, one on top of the other, into a tree.

MATERIALS
- clean half-gallon milk cartons
- colored construction paper
- crayons or markers
- clear self-adhesive paper
- scissors
- nails
- string

TOY TEST

Discuss the enormity of toys made of plastic and paper. Explain that just like plastic and paper food containers, we should try to use the toys for as long as possible and then recycle them. Explain the importance of choosing good quality toys that will not easily break. Discuss taking care of toys so they last longer and do not need to be replaced. Place five or six toys on a table. Include toys made of high-quality and low-quality fabric, wood, paper, or plastic. Divide the class into groups. Invite each group to observe the toys and rank them in order from best quality to worst quality. Invite the groups to share their rankings and tell why they made their choices. Then have them point out the best toy to buy. Remind students to make the same decisions when they go toy shopping.

MATERIALS

▲ wooden box

▲ leaves

▲ half-pound of red worms

▲ soil

▲ easily biodegradable vegetable waste

FALL COMPOST

Make a fall compost box to show students how to give back what they take from the earth. Ask parent volunteers to build one 2' x 2' (61 cm x 61 cm) wooden box that is approximately 8" (20.5 cm) deep. Place the box in a secluded outside location. Invite students to bring in raked leaves from home and fill the box with them. Purchase a half-pound of red worms at

a nursery or bait shop and place them in the leaves. Invite a student volunteer to place two handfuls of soil in the box. On a designated day, ask students to collect biodegradable vegetable waste from their school lunches (such as orange peels or apple cores) and place the waste in the box. Mix the contents of the box and wait several weeks. The worms will begin to do their work and make fertile soil from garbage!

TOMIE DE PAOLA'S BIRTHDAY

September 15

Tomie De Paola was born in 1934 in Meriden, Connecticut. When Tomie was a boy, he loved art and tap dancing. During his career in publishing, Tomie De Paola has written and/or illustrated more than 160 books. Help your students get to know the work of this fabulous artist and author with the following activities.

LITERATURE LINKS

Charlie Needs a Cloak
by Tomie De Paola

Helga's Dowry: A Troll Love Story
by Tomie De Paola

Nana Upstairs & Nana Downstairs
by Tomie De Paola

Now One Foot, Now the Other
by Tomie De Paola

Strega Nona
by Tomie De Paola

Tom
by Tomie De Paola

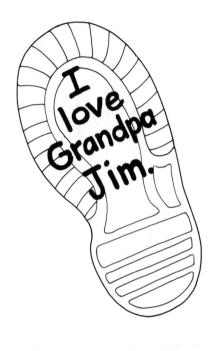

NOW ONE FOOT, NOW THE OTHER

Invite students to bring to school old shoes with interesting treads. Read aloud *Now One Foot, Now the Other*, the story of a grandfather and grandson's special relationship. Invite students to think of one skill a grandparent or an older friend has taught them, such as how to ride a bike or bake a pie. Have each student take out the old shoes, paint the treads with tempera paints, and stamp each shoe onto construction paper. (Students should immediately wash shoe bottoms after stamping.) Invite students to cut out the dry shoe prints. Have each student use black permanent marker on the left shoe print to write *My (grandfather, grandmother, friend) taught me to (skill)* and *I love (grandparent's name)* on the right shoe print. Tape the shoe prints along the wall so they look like footsteps. Add the heading *Taking Steps with Grandparents*.

MATERIALS

▲ *Now One Foot, Now the Other* by Tomie De Paola
▲ old shoes with interesting treads
▲ tempera paint
▲ construction paper
▲ scissors
▲ black permanent marker
▲ tape

MATERIALS

▲ *Strega Nona* by Tomie De Paola
▲ pasta
▲ pot
▲ water
▲ stove or hot plate
▲ apron
▲ bandanna or scarf
▲ wooden spoon
▲ large butcher-paper bar graph
▲ markers
▲ plastic bowls and forks
▲ pasta sauces

STREGA NONA COMES TO SCHOOL

Read aloud and discuss *Strega Nona* just before lunchtime. Explain that you heard that Strega Nona might be visiting your class after lunch. Cook a large pot of pasta while students are at lunch. Put on an apron and tie a bandanna or scarf around your head to become Strega Nona. When students return, stir the pot of pasta and invite students to recite the chant from the book. Place a small amount of pasta in a bowl for each child and invite students to choose one of three pasta sauces to place on top. Keep a tally of chosen sauces and graph the results on a large butcher-paper bar graph. (Students can write their names on index cards and tape them to the graph to show their favorite sauce.) Discuss the graph as students eat.

MATERIALS

▲ *Helga's Dowry: A Troll Love Story* by Tomie De Paola
▲ Crown Pattern (page63)
▲ crayons or markers
▲ scissors
▲ construction paper
▲ tagboard

HELGA'S NEW DOWRY

Read aloud *Helga's Dowry: A Troll Love Story*. Explain the word *dowry* and ask each student to think of a positive personality trait or caring action Helga the Troll could offer a fiancé as a dowry. Reproduce the crown pattern on construction paper, one crown for each student. Invite students to draw their own version of Helga on a crown. Have students complete the following sentence frame under their picture: *My name is Helga and I am so smart. I offer _____ as my dowry and also my heart.* Bind the pages in a tagboard cover titled *Helga's Dowry for the King.*

My name is Helga and I am so smart.
I offer honesty as my dowry
and also my heart.   Tasha

CROWN

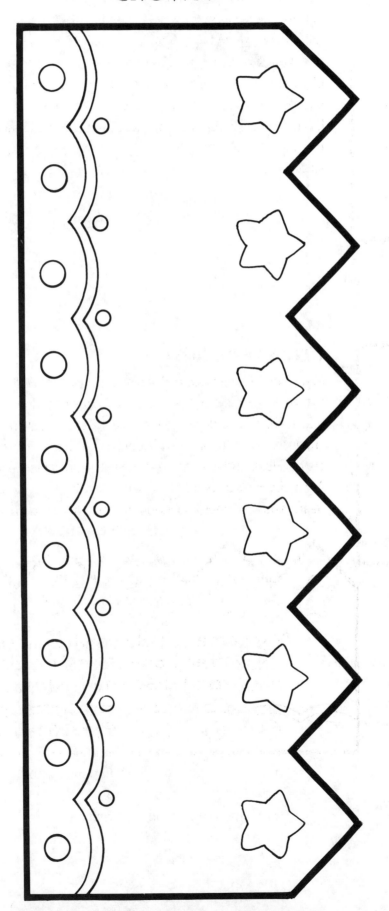

Bill of Rights

CITIZENSHIP DAY

The United States Constitution was ratified on September 17, 1787. Delegates from 12 of the 13 original colonies met in Philadelphia to write what would become one of the most important documents in our country's history. Celebrate Citizenship Day with your students to help them understand the importance of rights and responsibilities . . . in the classroom and their country!

LITERATURE LINKS

The Bill of Rights
by Warren Colman

The Constitution
by Warren Colman

If You Were There When They Signed the Constitution
by Elizabeth Levy

Responsibility
by Glenn Alan Cheney

We the People: The Constitution of the United States of America
by Peter Spier

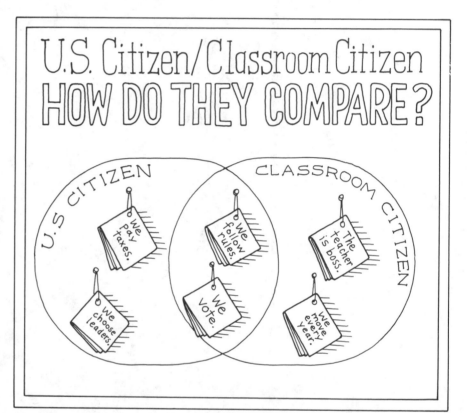

U.S. Citizen/Classroom Citizen
HOW DO THEY COMPARE?

U.S CITIZEN — CLASSROOM CITIZEN

We pay taxes. / We follow rules. / The teacher is boss. / We choose leaders. / We vote. / We move every year.

CITIZENSHIP BULLETIN BOARD

Staple a large Venn diagram made of thick yarn to a bulletin board labeled *U.S. Citizen/Classroom Citizen—How Do They Compare?* As a class, brainstorm the similarities and differences between being a citizen of a classroom and a citizen of a country. Divide the class into groups and assign one of the brainstormed similarities or differences to each group. Have each student illustrate and write on an index card the similarity or difference. Ask each student to punch a hole in the top left corner of the index cards. Tie each group's cards together with a string. Invite each group to staple their cards in the correct place on the Venn diagram.

MATERIALS
▲ thick yarn
▲ index cards
▲ scissors
▲ crayons or makers
▲ hole punch
▲ string

CITIZENSHIP BUTTONS

MATERIALS

▲ construction paper circles
▲ chart paper
▲ crayons or markers
▲ laminator
▲ hole punch
▲ safety pins

Have each student design a construction paper circle "citizenship button" and write his or her name in the center. Discuss the qualities of a good citizen in both the classroom and society and record descriptive words on chart paper. Ask each student to choose four words that describe himself or herself and write them inside the button. Invite students to decorate the buttons with crayons or markers. Laminate the buttons. Have students punch two holes in the top of the button and thread a safety pin through the holes. Invite students to wear the buttons in the classroom on Citizenship Day.

CLASS BILL OF RIGHTS

MATERIALS

▲ poster board
▲ crayons or markers

Explain that the Bill of Rights is the part of the United States Constitution that lists the rights citizens have. Give an example, such as *Citizens have the right to say what they wish (free speech).* As a class, brainstorm a Class Bill of Rights. Have students think of a responsibility that correlates with each right. For example, if students have the right to learn, then they have the responsibility to listen so they and others can hear the teacher. List each right/responsibility pair on a different piece of poster board. Divide the class into groups. Invite each group to illustrate the right/responsibility. Hang the posters to remind students of their rights and responsibilities during school.

FOOTBALL DAY

September 17

The National Football League was founded on September 17, 1920. Invite students to celebrate this traditional autumn sport by having them complete the following Football Day activities; they'll "have a ball"!

LITERATURE LINKS

The Dallas Titans Get Ready for Bed
by Karla Kuskin

Football
by Ray Broekel

Louanne Pig Is Making the Team
by Nancy Carlson

Sidney Rella and the Glass Sneaker
by Bernice Myers

Snail Saves the Day
by John Stadler

MAPPING THE TEAMS BULLETIN BOARD

Teach geography with this fun activity. Divide the class into groups. Invite each group to pick a different NFL team as their team for the season. Staple a large United States map to a bulletin board. Invite each group to decorate and cutout a Football Helmet for their team and pin it to the board to show its team's hometown. Each weekend, ask students to check the local papers to find out where their teams are playing the following week. On Monday, invite a student from each group to tell if his or her team is playing "at home" or tell the "away" location and move the team's helmet to the location in which it will play. For extra fun, track the teams' wins and losses throughout the season.

MATERIALS
▲ NFL Team List (see page 68)
▲ large United States map
▲ Football Helmet (page 68)
▲ tacks or pushpins

FOOTBALL RELAY

Divide the class into four evenly numbered groups. Take the class to an open playing area. Have each group stand at a chalk or tape starting line, one student behind another. Have the first player on each team hold a football between his or her knees without using hands. Say *Go* and have the first players walk with the football between their knees to a turnaround line, walk back to the starting line, and give the football to the second players. Continue the relay until each student has had a turn. The first team to have all players return to the starting line is the winner. For extra fun, have another relay in which teams (standing in line) pass the football alternating between their legs and overhead.

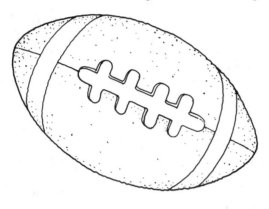

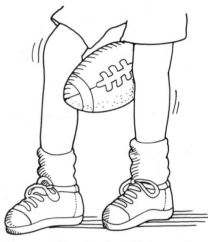

FOOTBALL MEASUREMENT

Discuss the importance of yards in a football game. Give football facts, such as *A football field is 100 yards long, A football field is 50 yards wide, The most popular seats at a football game are on the 50-yard line (because of the view),* and *A team needs to move the ball 10 yards to get a "first down."* Take the class to the playground. As a class, estimate and then measure 10, 50, and 100 yards with yardsticks. For extra fun, mark 100 yards by placing a traffic cone at each end of the measurement. Invite students to sprint from one cone to the other to gain an understanding of the endurance a football player needs.

This is 10 yards.

That's far!

NFL TEAM LIST

American Football Conference

Eastern Division
Buffalo Bills
Indianapolis Colts
Miami Dolphins
New England Patriots
New York Jets

Central Division
Cincinnati Bengals
Baltimore Ravens
Tennessee Oilers
Jacksonville Jaguars
Pittsburgh Steelers

Western Division
Denver Broncos
Kansas City Chiefs
Oakland Raiders
San Diego Chargers
Seattle Seahawks

National Football Conference

Eastern Division
Arizona Cardinals
Dallas Cowboys
New York Giants
Philadelphia Eagles
Washington Redskins

Central Division
Chicago Bears
Detroit Lions
Green Bay Packers
Minnesota Vikings
Tampa Bay Buccaneers

Western Division
Atlanta Falcons
Carolina Panthers
New Orleans Saints
St. Louis Rams
San Francisco 49ers

FOOTBALL HELMET

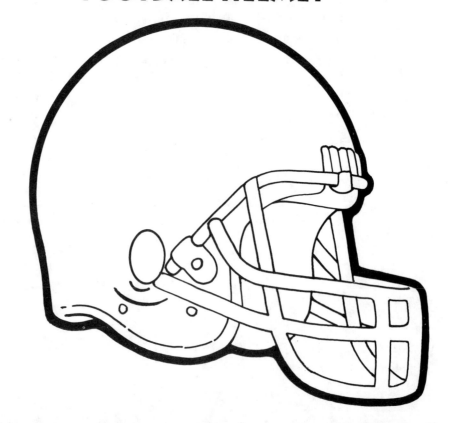

September © 1998 Creative Teaching Press

FABULOUS FALL DAY

October is great.
October is fun.
Trick or treats
for
everyone!

Autumn leaf,
Falling down.
Watch you
Tumble
to the
Ground.

First Day of Autumn

The first day of Autumn, the Autumnal Equinox, falls in the third week of September. Invite your students to enjoy the following fall activities to celebrate the change of seasons. Your students will see that autumn is awesome!

LITERATURE LINKS

Autumn
by Ralph Whitlock

Autumn
by Richard L. Allington

Autumn Days
by Ann Schweninger

Autumn Story
by Jill Barklem

*The Cinnamon Hen's
Autumn Day*
by Sandra Dutton

Follow the Fall
by Maxine Kumin

Now It's Fall
by Lois Lenski

FABULOUS FALL "PO-E-TREE"

Brainstorm and record with the class a list of autumn activities, colors, feelings, and games. Invite each student to use the words to compose a fall poem with a specific rhyme scheme such as an *ABB* pattern, an *ABCB* pattern, or a rhyming couplet pattern. Help students revise their poems and write them in the center of a Leaf Pattern. Invite students to sponge-paint with fall colors around the perimeter of the leaves and cut them out. Have each student share his or her poem and then tape it to a twisted butcher paper tree that has been stapled to a classroom or hallway corner.

MATERIALS
▲ writing paper
▲ Leaf Pattern (page 45)
▲ sponges
▲ tempera paint in fall colors
▲ brown butcher paper

AUTUMN ARITHMETIC LEARNING CENTER

MATERIALS
▲ Leaf Pattern (page 45)
▲ 8 1/2" x 11" (21.5 cm x 28 cm) sheets of construction paper
▲ 55 dry white beans
▲ red spray paint
▲ laminator
▲ dry-erase markers

Write a number name and numeral symbol (from one to ten) on ten individual Leaf Patterns and then laminate the pages to make ten "leaf sheets." Paint 55 dry white beans with red spray paint so one side is red. Place the beans and leaf sheets in a learning center. Have students who visit the center lay out the leaf sheets in order from one to ten. Ask students to place the corresponding number of beans on each leaf sheet so the red sides show. (They will use all 55 beans.) Have students flip over one bean on each leaf sheet so the white side is showing. Have students use dry-erase marker to write an addition problem on each sheet to correspond with the number and color of beans on it. (For example, on the "five" leaf sheet, a student would have four red beans and one white bean and write $4 + 1 = 5$.) Then students erase the equations and flip another bean on each sheet to show two white beans on each. Instruct students to write new equations for two white beans. (Students would write $3 + 2 = 5$ on the "five" leaf sheet). Students will notice that they cannot flip two beans on the "one" leaf sheet; they should then eliminate that sheet (put it away). Have students continue flipping beans, writing equations, and eliminating sheets until all beans are flipped.

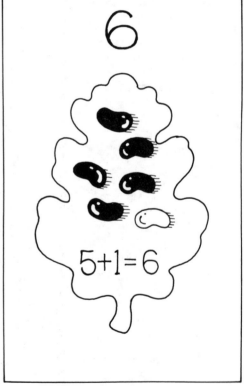

ICE-CREAM CONE DAY

National Ice-Cream Cone Day is celebrated on September 22 to commemorate the invention of the ice-cream cone. Invite your students to get a "taste" of some fun ice-cream activities—they're "cool"!

LITERATURE LINKS

"Bleezer's Ice Cream" from *The New Kid on the Block* by Jack Prelutsky

Curious George Goes to An Ice-Cream Shop by Carolyn Croll

Ice Cream by William Jaspersohn

"Ice Cream" from *Frog and Toad All Year* by Arnold Lobel

Ice Creams for Rosie by Ronda Armitage

The Land Where the Ice Cream Grows by Fulvio Testa

ICE-CREAM CONE CLOWNS

Place a scoop of ice cream on a cupcake liner for each student. Place the scoops and liners on individual paper plates. Invite students to place a pointed sugar cone on top of the scoop to make a hat. Have students decorate a clown face under the hat using jelly beans, M&Ms, and licorice strings. Invite students to eat and enjoy while listening to an ice-cream story.

MATERIALS

▲ vanilla or chocolate ice cream

▲ cupcake liners

▲ pointed sugar cones

▲ jelly beans, M&Ms, licorice strings

▲ ice-cream story (see Literature Links)

MATERIALS

▲ ice-cream toppings (chocolate chips, marshmallows, M&Ms, raisins, nuts, chocolate syrup, caramel syrup, and strawberry preserves)
▲ Price Sheet (page 71)
▲ bowls
▲ real or plastic coins
▲ plastic sandwich bags
▲ ice cream
▲ plastic bowls

MATERIALS

▲ "Bleezer's Ice Cream" from *The New Kid on the Block* by Jack Prelutsky
▲ 8 1/2" x 11" (21.5 cm x 28 cm) colored construction paper
▲ colored construction paper
▲ 9" x 12" (23 cm x 30.5 cm) light-brown construction paper
▲ crayons or markers
▲ scissors
▲ glue

GOURMET ICE-CREAM STORE

Set up a "gourmet ice-cream store" by placing on a table the ice-cream toppings listed on the Price Sheet. Divide the class into pairs. Invite each pair to complete a Price Sheet to show their topping choices for an ice-cream treat. Have pairs use $1.00 in real or plastic coins to figure out how much they will spend. Then have pairs bring a bowl and a plastic sandwich bag with the coins to the "store." Have pairs place their chosen toppings in the bowl and pay for them with the coins. Provide each student with a plastic bowl of ice cream and invite him or her to add the chosen toppings and eat!

SILLY ICE-CREAM CONES

Read aloud "Bleezer's Ice Cream"; then invite students to make their own silly ice-cream flavors. Invite each student to think of a new flavor such as fish and worm ice cream. Have students crumple colored construction paper into three balls to make "ice-cream scoops." Ask students to cover the scoops with construction paper cutouts decorated to represent their new flavor. Have each student cut off one edge of a light-brown piece of construction paper. Ask students to roll the paper into a cone shape so the rounded edge is on top and tape it closed. Have students place their ice-cream scoops into the cone. Invite each student to hold his or her cone, explain the new flavor, and try to convince the class that it is delicious. Have the class vote for the most-delicious and least-delicious flavors.

Fish N' Worms
LEAST DELICIOUS AWARD

~~~~~~

PRICE SHEET

Names _____

Welcome to the Gourmet Ice-Cream Store! You have $1.00 to spend on toppings. Choose the toppings you like. Then complete the questions.

Chocolate Chips	Marshmallows	M&Ms	Raisins
$ .15 per scoop	$ .10 per scoop	$ .15 per scoop	$ .10 per scoop
Nuts	Chocolate Syrup	Caramel Syrup	Strawberry Preserves
$ .10 per scoop	$ .20 per spoonful	$ .20 per spoonful	$ .20 per spoonful

1. What toppings did you decide to buy? _____

_____

2. How much of each topping?

Number of Scoops	Number of Scoops/Spoonfuls x Price per Scoop/Spoonful	Total Price
____ scoops of _____	_____ x $. _____	$ _____
____ scoops of _____	_____ x $. _____	$ _____
____ scoops of _____	_____ x $. _____	$ _____
____ scoops of _____	_____ x $. _____	$ _____
____ scoops of _____	_____ x $. _____	$ _____
____ spoonfuls of _____	_____ x $. _____	$ _____
____ spoonfuls of _____	_____ x $. _____	$ _____
____ spoonfuls of _____	_____ x $. _____	$ _____

3. Add all the total prices. How much money will you spend? _____

4. Subtract the total from $1.00. How much money will you have left? _____

MUPPET DAY

Jim Henson, creator of the muppets, was born on September 24, 1936 in Greensville, Missouri. Sesame Street, which features the delightful muppets, has delighted and educated millions for more than 20 years. You can celebrate Jim Henson's birthday with the following Muppet Day activities. Your students are sure to relate to the characters and have a great time!

LITERATURE LINKS

Big Bird's Big Bike
by Anna Ross

Big Bird's Farm
by the Sesame Street Staff

*Cookie Monster,
Where Are You?*
by the Sesame Street Staff

*Cookie Monster's
Good Time to Eat!*
by Richard Brown

Elmo's Little Playhouse
by Anna Ross

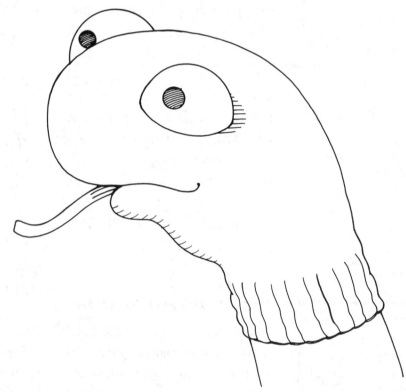

FROG SOCK PUPPETS

Have each student bring in an old white sock from home. Dye the socks with green fabric dye and let dry. Invite each student to cut a Styrofoam ball in half and draw a black pupil on each half for "frog eyes." Ask each student to put the sock on one hand (thumb in sock heel) and draw an *X* where each "frog eye" should be placed. Have students glue the eyes in place and remove the socks. Invite students to cut red felt "tongues" and glue them just above the sock heel where the "frog mouth" opens and closes. Invite students to use their frog puppets to act out a "Kermit song."

MATERIALS

▲ old white socks
▲ green fabric dye and dyeing materials
▲ 1"-diameter (2.5 cm-diameter) Styrofoam balls
▲ permanent marker
▲ red felt
▲ scissors
▲ fabric glue
▲ "Kermit song" (such as "The Rainbow Connection" from *The Muppet Movie* soundtrack)

COOKIE MONSTER MATH

MATERIALS

▲ small paper lunch sacks
▲ crayons or markers
▲ blue yarn or blue craft fur
▲ wiggly eyes
▲ construction-paper mouths
▲ glue
▲ Cookie Crisp cereal

Invite each student to draw a Cookie Monster on a small paper lunch sack. Have students cover their monster with blue yarn or blue craft fur and glue on wiggly eyes and a construction-paper mouth. Give each student several Cookie Crisp cereal "cookies." Tell a subtraction story and have students use the cookies and the lunch sack monsters to show the problems. For example, you might say, *Cookie Monster had seven cookies. He gobbled three cookies. How many were left?* Students should count out seven cookies, place three in the lunch sack, and have four cookies left in front of them. Tell several stories; then invite students to take the sacks home and play the game with their families.

BIG BIRD'S MIGRATION

MATERIALS

▲ world map
▲ 8 1/2" x 11" (21.5 cm x 28 cm) white construction paper
▲ crayons or markers
▲ yellow craft feathers
▲ wiggly eyes
▲ candy corn
▲ glue

Discuss how birds, in preparation for winter, migrate in autumn from North to South. Invite students to pretend they are Big Bird, look at a world map, and choose a place south of where they live to migrate. Invite each student to complete the following sentence frame on the bottom of a piece of white construction paper: *My name is Big Bird and winter is near. I'll move to _____ until spring is here.* Have students glue a large yellow craft feather in the center of the paper to illustrate their sentences. Ask students to glue wiggly eyes on the feather near the top. Next have students glue a candy-corn beak under the eyes. Finally, invite students to draw yellow wings on either side of

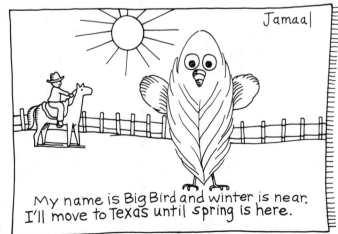

Jamaal

My name is Big Bird and winter is near. I'll move to Texas until spring is here.

the feather and draw feet under the feather. Have students surround the Big Bird with a scene from their chosen destination. Display the papers on a wall near the heading *Big Bird's Migration*.

JOHNNY APPLESEED DAY

John Chapman, also known as Johnny Appleseed, was an American pioneer who planted apple orchards in the frontiers of Pennsylvania, Ohio, Indiana, and Illinois. The legends about his love of animals, friendships with Native Americans, and interesting clothing (a pot on his head) have made him a folk hero. You can celebrate Johnny's contribution to our harvest table with the following yummy activities!

LITERATURE LINKS

Apple Tree! Apple Tree!
by Mary Blocksma

Johnny Appleseed
by Steven Kellogg

Johnny Appleseed
by Reeve Lindbergh

The Seasons of Arnold's Apple Tree
by Gail Gibbons

The Story of Johnny Appleseed
by Aliki

apple-sauce	Rachel, Don
apple juice	Amy, Vince, Jill
apple pie	Caleb, Matt, Gary, Val, Ellen
dried apple chips	Grace, Kim, Brian
apple slices	Sonya, James

GRAPHING APPLES

Explain that Johnny Appleseed is a folk hero known for planting apple orchards throughout the United States. Invite students to brainstorm the "fruits" of Johnny's contribution by naming foods made from apples. Divide the class into groups and give each group several "apple food" samples, such as applesauce, apple juice, apple pie, dried apple chips, and apple slices. Invite students to taste each food and choose a favorite. Have each student cut out an apple shape, write his or her name on it, and tape it to a class graph to show his or her favorite. Discuss the graph as a class.

MATERIALS

▲ foods made from apples (applesauce, apple juice, apple pie, dried apple chips, apple slices)

▲ cups, plates, napkins, plastic forks

▲ class graph showing each food

▲ Clip Art apple shape (page 95)

MATERIALS

▲ 8 1/2" x 11" (21. 5 cm x 28 cm) white construction paper
▲ crayons or markers
▲ bookbinding materials

JOHNNY APPLESEED CLASS BOOK

Discuss names for apples such as Macintosh, Granny Smith, Golden Delicious, and Fuji. Invite each student to invent a new variety of apple and give it an interesting name. For example, a child might invent an apple that grows to be as large as a pumpkin and give it the name Jack-O'-Apple. Invite each student to illustrate his or her idea on white construction paper and write the name under the drawing. Compile the pages in a class book titled *Apple Seeds Johnny Forgot to Plant!*

APPLE "PIZZA"

Make the following recipe as a class to celebrate Johnny Appleseed's contribution to our dessert tables.

MATERIALS

▲ 3–4 tubes refrigerated biscuit dough
▲ butter
▲ apple slices
▲ sugar
▲ cinnamon
▲ raisins
▲ cookie sheets
▲ nonstick cooking spray

1. Have each student flatten a biscuit from refrigerated biscuit dough into a 1/2"-thick (1 cm-thick) pizza shape.
2. Have students place their "pizza" on a cookie sheet sprayed with nonstick cooking spray.
3. Invite students to spread a small amount of butter on the dough.
4. Ask each student to place three or four apple slices on top, and then sprinkle with sugar and cinnamon.
5. Have students top the dough with three or four raisins.
6. Bake the "pizzas" at 375° for 8 to 10 minutes.
7. Let cool and serve.

NATIVE AMERICAN DAY

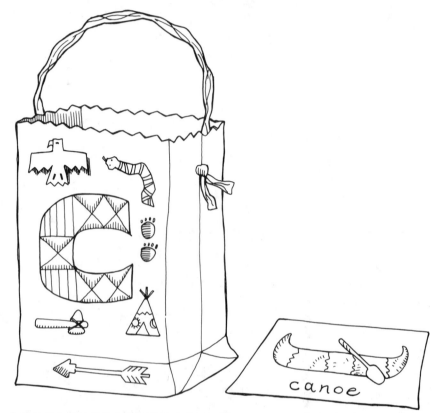

canoe

Fourth Friday

Native American Day is celebrated the fourth Friday of September. You and your students can pay tribute to the important contributions of our nation's first settlers with the following activities.

LITERATURE LINKS

Brother Eagle, Sister Sky: A message from Chief Seattle Illustrated by Susan Jeffers

Children of the Earth and Sky by Stephen Krensky

Children of the Wind and Water by Stephen Krensky

Dancing with the Indians by Angela Shelf Medeair

The Mud Pony retold by Caron Lee Cohen

The Path of the Quiet Elk (A Native American Alphabet Book) by Virginia A. Stroud

ABC SACK LEARNING CENTER

Read aloud and discuss *The Path of the Quiet Elk.* Have students brainstorm another Native American item or item from nature that begins with each letter of the alphabet, such as antelope for *A*, baskets for *B*, and canoe for *C*. (Use the object from the book for letter *X*.) Invite each student to choose a letter, illustrate and label the corresponding item on drawing paper, and set the illustration aside. Next have each student decorate a lunch sack with Native American designs. Ask students to write their assigned letter on the sacks. Punch handle holes in either side of the sacks, and have students tie on a raffia handle. Invite students to place their illustrations inside the sacks and hang the sacks on a yarn "clothesline." Invite students to visit the "clothesline," guess the names of the illustrations inside the sacks, and pull out the illustrations to check their predictions.

MATERIALS
- ▲ *The Path of the Quiet Elk (A Native American Alphabet Book)* by Virginia A. Stroud
- ▲ 5" x 7" (12.5 cm x 17.5 cm) drawing paper
- ▲ crayons or markers
- ▲ small lunch sacks
- ▲ hole punch
- ▲ raffia
- ▲ yarn

NATIVE AMERICAN STICK GAME

MATERIALS
▲ craft sticks
▲ red spray paint
▲ Stick Game Score Card reproducible (page 83)

Invite students to play a traditional Native American children's game. Obtain three craft sticks for each student and paint one side of the sticks red. Divide students into four or five groups. Invite players in each group, one at a time, to hold the three sticks in their fist and drop them. Students get one point for each red side that shows and no points for an unpainted side. Have groups play four rounds. Ask each student to keep track of his or her score by coloring sticks on the Stick Game Score Card with red crayon and writing points next to them. The player with the most points in each group is the winner. Send the sticks home so students can play with their families.

DECORATED "BUFFALO HIDE"

MATERIALS
▲ large grocery sacks
▲ 2" x 24" (5 cm x 61 cm) cardboard strips
▲ crayons or markers
▲ Pictographs (page 84)
▲ hole punch
▲ yarn
▲ stapler
▲ scissors

Invite each student to cut out and use one side from a large grocery sack. Have students tear the four edges to create a rough-edged "buffalo hide." Ask students to draw a story from the Pictographs to decorate the hide. Have students punch holes around the outer edge of the hide. Ask students to place four cardboard strips in a rectangle around the hide so there is a 2" (5 cm) gap between the strips and the hide. Have students staple the cardboard "frame" in place. Invite students to "sew" through the holes and around the cardboard frame as shown. Hang the hides for display.

Names _____

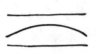

STICK GAME SCORE CARD

Round One

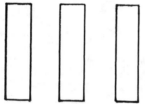

= _____ points

Round Two

= _____ points

Round Three

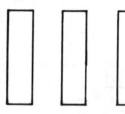

= _____ points

Round Four

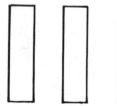

= _____ points

September © 1998 Creative Teaching Press

PICTOGRAPHS

 Indian camp

 brother

 make peace

 bird tracks

deer

 council

 talk together

 wise man

 hunt

 river

lake

 teepee

 hear

 spirit

 eat

 beaver

 horse tracks

 Campfire

 look

 rain

 cold and snow

 three days

 three nights

 morning

 noon

evening

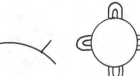 North

 hungry

fear

September © 1998 Creative Teaching Press

NATIONAL FISHING DAY

Fourth Saturday

National Fishing Day is celebrated on the fourth Saturday of September. Bring out the "angler" in your students with the following "fishy" activities; they're a great catch!

LITERATURE LINKS

The Little Fisherman
by Margaret Wise Brown

Nathan's Fishing Trip
by LuLu Delacre

The Rainbow Fish
by Marcus Pfister

The Fisherman and His Wife
retold by Eric Carle (from *Eric Carle's Treasury of Classic Stories for Children*)

What Is a Fish?
by David Eastman

FISHING FOR FRIENDSHIP

Invite each student to write inside a Fish Pattern three or four qualities that make him or her a good friend. For example, a student might write *I am a good listener; I like to play one-on-one basketball;* and *I share my school supplies.* Invite students to color the patterns in their two favorite colors as a clue to their identity. Ask students to cut out the patterns and write their names on the back. Attach a paper clip to each fish and clip the fish vertically on three 2'-long (61 cm-long) yarn pieces to make three "strings of fish." Hang the strings of fish on a bulletin board titled *Guess Who Was Caught Being a Good Friend!* Invite students to visit the bulletin-board learning center, read the qualities on several fish, and guess whom the fish are describing. Students can self-check by reading the backs of the fish.

MATERIALS
▲ Fish Pattern (page 84)
▲ scissors
▲ crayons or markers
▲ yarn
▲ paper clips

THE FISHERMAN AND HIS WIFE

MATERIALS

▲ *The Fisherman and His Wife* retold by Eric Carle (from *Eric Carle's Treasury of Classic Stories for Children*)

▲ Fish Pattern (page 87)

▲ aluminum foil

▲ scissors

▲ glue

▲ crayons or markers

▲ hole punch

▲ yarn

Read aloud and discuss Eric Carle's version of *The Fisherman and His Wife*. Invite students to brainstorm wishes they might ask the fish in the story. Have each student write his or her wish in the center of the Fish Pattern. Ask students to cut out aluminum foil scales and glue them over several scales on the pattern. Have students color the fish and cut them out. Punch holes in the fish and hang them from the ceiling near the heading *If You Caught the Fish, What Would You Wish?*

FISHING FOR WORDS POCKET-CHART ACTIVITY

MATERIALS

▲ Fish Pattern (page 87)

▲ large paper clips

▲ tape

▲ large tub

▲ yardstick or meter stick

▲ string

▲ magnet

Cut out a Fish Pattern for each student and tape a large paper clip to each fish. Print a vocabulary word (from a current topic of study or reading lesson) on each fish. Place the fish in a large tub. Tape a 3' (91.5 cm) string to the end of a yardstick or a meter stick as a "fishing pole." Tie a magnet to the end of the string. Invite each student to toss the "line" from the fishing pole into the tub to fish for a word. Invite students to "reel in" a fish that becomes attached to the magnet, read the word on it aloud, and place the fish inside the pocket chart. After all fish are caught and in the pocket chart, read the words as a group.

FISH PATTERN

National Fishing Day

September © 1998 Creative Teaching Press

GOOD-NEIGHBOR DAY

The fourth Sunday in September is National Good-Neighbor Day. And since September also marks the beginning of a new school year, it's the perfect time to study your school's neighborhood and the importance of being a good neighbor in the classroom and in society. Involve your students in the following activities — they're fun and friendly!

LITERATURE LINKS

Country Bear's Good Neighbor
by Larry Dane

Good Neighbors
by Diane Redfield Massie

Loudmouth George and His New Neighbors
by Nancy Carlson

My Perfect Neighborhood
by Leah Komaiko

Once around the Block
by Kevin Henkes

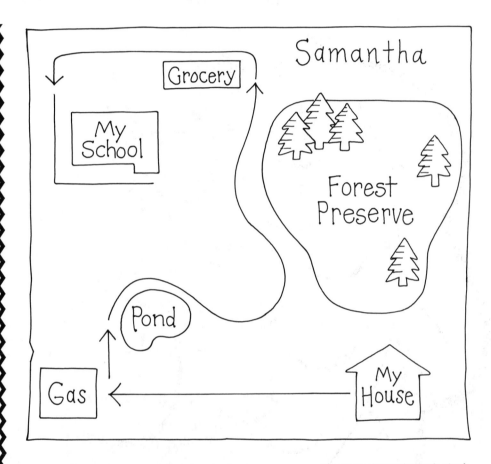

NEIGHBORHOOD MAPS

This fun activity will help students remember the route they take to school. Bring in several identical maps of your community. Divide the class into groups and give each a map. Have a class discussion of your community and invite each student to find his or her street on the map. Have students use the community maps as a reference and draw their own map to show how they get to school each day. Invite students to add significant personal landmarks and color their maps. Display the maps under the heading *Our Neighborhoods from Home to School.*

MATERIALS
▲ community maps
▲ 12" x 18" (30.5 cm x 46 cm) drawing paper
▲ crayons or markers

MATERIALS

▲ student-made invitations

SCHOOL "AMBASSADORS"

Discuss the need to be good neighbors to people who live and work near your school and in your community. Ask your class to become "ambassadors" for the school and invite the school's neighbors to attend an event such as Back-to-School Night or the first musical or dramatic performance of the year. Have each student make an invitation to the event. Take the class on a "neighborhood walk" and invite students to leave their invitations at the door of homes and businesses.

MATERIALS

▲ Good-Neighbor Award Letter (page 88)

GOOD-NEIGHBOR AWARDS

Send home a Good-Neighbor Award Letter with each student the night before National Good-Neighbor Day. (The letter invites parents to share how their son or daughter is a good neighbor.) Ask students to return parent responses the next day. Collect the responses and read aloud the words their parents wrote as you present the awards.

GOOD-NEIGHBOR AWARD

Dear Family,

We are celebrating National Good-Neighbor Day at school, and we'd like to include you in the festivities! Think about your child's respect for others in your neighborhood and complete the Good-Neighbor Award below. Please return the award tomorrow so your child can receive it with the rest of the class. Happy National Good-Neighbor Day!

Good-Neighbor Award

I'm proud of my child _____!

_____

was a good neighbor when

_____

_____

_____

Congratulations and keep up the good work!

HARVEST MOON DAY

There is something magical about the moon in autumn. Unlike autumn on Earth, the moon has no weather, no clouds, no rain, and no wind! Treat your students to the wonders of the moon with the following moon activities—they're out of this world!

LITERATURE LINKS

Goodnight Moon
by Margaret Wise Brown

Moon
by Seymour Simon

Moon by Night
by Madeleine L'Engle

Moondance
by Frank Asch

Moonlight
by Jan Ormerod

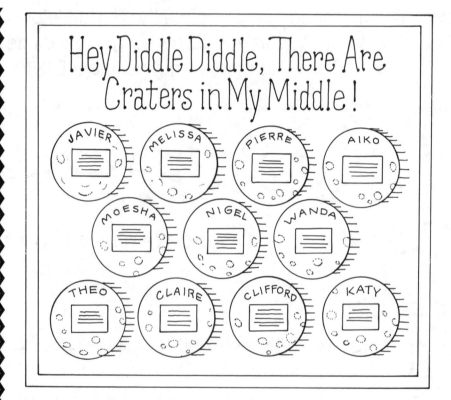

Hey Diddle Diddle, There Are Craters in My Middle!

JAVIER MELISSA PIERRE AIKO

MOESHA NIGEL WANDA

THEO CLAIRE CLIFFORD KATY

MAKE A MOON BULLETIN BOARD

Explain that the moon is covered with craters that were made by flying debris that landed on it and left holes in its surface. Have students glue small objects to small paper plates to create their own crater-filled moons. Ask students to cover the plates with aluminum foil and mold the foil to the plates so the surface is bumpy. Reproduce "Hey Diddle Diddle" on 3" x 5" (7.5 cm x 12.5 cm) index cards for each student and have students glue the rhyme in the center of their moon. Display the moons on a bulletin board titled *Hey Diddle Diddle, There Are Craters in My Middle!*

MATERIALS

▲ small paper plates
▲ small objects such as pebbles or dry macaroni
▲ glue
▲ aluminum foil
▲ "Hey Diddle Diddle" nursery rhyme
▲ 3" x 5" (7.5 cm x 12.5 cm) index cards

WANING AND WAXING MOONS

Have each student divide a piece of black construction paper into eight equal-size sections. Have students write in each section a different phase of the moon: *new moon, waxing crescent, first quarter, waxing gibbous, full moon, waning gibbous, last quarter, waning crescent*. Explain that these words represent what the moon looks like from Earth during every month as the moon revolves around the Earth. Have students leave the "new moon square" blank because the term *new moon* refers to the time of the month when no moon is visible in the sky. Have students draw a white chalk moon or white crayon moon in the remaining squares to represent each phase. (See the illustration examples.) Invite students to look at the sky each night in September to find the moon as it goes from phase to phase.

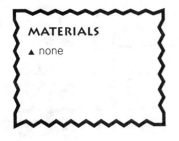

			Ronald
new moon	waxing crescent	first quarter	waxing gibbous
full moon	waning gibbous	last quarter	waning crescent

ORBIT, ORBIT, LITTLE MOON

Have students hold hands and stand in a circle. (These students represent the moon's orbit.) Ask one student to stand in the center of the circle. (This student represents the Earth.) Invite the class to sing the following song as they walk around the "Earth." Have the "Earth student" stand and slowly spin in place to demonstrate the Earth's 24-hour revolution. Remind students that in addition to these movements, the moon and Earth are also orbiting around the sun.

Orbit, Orbit, Little Moon
(to the tune of "Twinkle, Twinkle, Little Star")

Orbit, orbit, little moon.
In the sky like a balloon.

Round the earth you like to spin.
Gone and then you're back again.

Orbit, orbit, in the sky.
Moon is floating, passing by.

SUNDAY	MONDAY	TUESDAY	WEDNESDAY	THURSDAY	FRIDAY	SATURDAY

SEPTEMBER

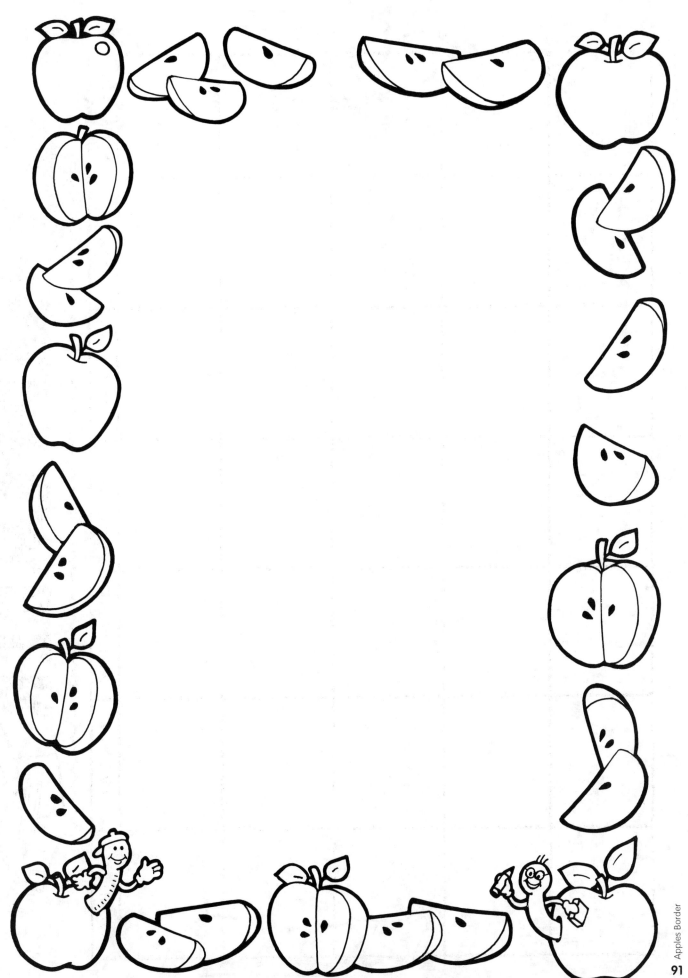

September News

September © 1998 Creative Teaching Press